You are
all Sanpaku

You are
all
Sanpaku

You are all Sanpaku

By Sakurazawa Nyoiti

English Version By William Dufty

You are
all
Sanpaku

A Citadel Press Book
Published by Carol Publishing Group

FOR

Brigitte Bardot

Harry Belafonte

Marc Bohan

Vincent L. Broderick

Willy Brandt

Sid Caesar

Michael Chaplin

Roy Cohn

Joe Curran

Bette Davis

Emile Di Antonio

Maely Daniele Dufty

Mark A. Fein

J. Paul Getty

Stan Getz

John Gielgud

Jackie Gleason

Günter Grass

J. Edgar Hoover

Anna Kashfi

Sen. Edward Kennedy

Sen. Robert Kennedy

Millard Lampell

Eric Leinsdorf

Dorothy Malone

Rep. Adam Clayton Powell

Barbara Powers

Gabe Pressman

Edward G. Robinson, Jr.

Françoise Sagan

Saroya

Robert Vaughn

Herbert Von Karajan

Capt. Eldridge Waith

Natalie Wood

Charles E. Wright

AND ALL THOSE WHO ARE SANPAKU

CONTENTS

Introduction

Why *then?* Why *there?*
Why *thus,* we cry, did he die?
The heavens are silent.

W. H. AUDEN

The death of President Kennedy changed many lives and begat many books, including, strange as it may seem, this one.

Auden asks the enduring question — the question beyond the ones which kept us glued to television for November days on end and kept us reading the unending torrent of words in our newspapers and magazines. One of the rare newspaper stories of those days which went beyond the obvious official facts of the tragedy and came to grips, however obliquely, with the unanswerables, appeared in the New York Herald Tribune Sunday Magazine of January 12, 1964, under the by-line of Tom Wolfe. Nothing in its title "Sanpaku On Second Avenue" would lead one to believe it had anything to do with Dallas at all. Its first sentence, however, was an eye-stopper.

> "Abdul Karim Kassem, President Ngo Dinh Diem and President Kennedy; all *sanpaku* and, now, all shot to death, all destroyed by the fate of the sanpaku, which is more than coincidence and should be an alarm signal to men and nations, say the Macrobiotics, for thus it has been demonstrated by their leader, George Ohsawa, Japanese prophet of the Unique Principle."

As a reformed journalist myself, acutely conscious of the limitations of the craft, I raced through several disjointed paragraphs with a rather practiced editorial eye. In somewhat ambivalent fashion, it told of a rather droll gathering of people eating kasha, rice, fish and sesame salt on Lower Second Avenue, with a flashback relating this in some way to the exodus of some other New Yorkers who fled Long Island in 1961 for Chico, California to escape atomic blast. But what is the fate of the sanpaku? Who is this extraordinary Japanese prophet? At the tail end of the story, on another page, it was explained that sanpaku means "not only illness of the body but a dangerous condition of the spirit and the psyche. The sanpaku man's entire system is out of balance, and he will be prone to accidents and tragic death...white showing beneath the iris of the eyes... (denotes) the condition known as sanpaku."

"Last August," the strange story continued, "George Ohsawa sat in his suite at the Wentworth Hotel with photographs of the great and celebrated spread out before him on the coffee table, Marilyn Monroe, Brigitte Bardot, Karim Kassem, President Diem and President Kennedy, among others. President Kennedy would suffer many severe difficulties in the near future, he told a reporter, and what he spoke of privately, his followers say, was a tragic end."

A reporter? *What* reporter? Did this remarkable forecast of the assassination of three heads of state ever appear in print? President Kennedy was one of the most avid newspaper readers around — had he read the prophecy? How about his doctors? The Secret Service? Clearly the story raised more questions than it answered. It concluded with the direct quotation of a message from the Japanese prophet who, it was said, had predicted the death of Gandhi, the death of Hitler, the end of British colonialism in India, and had been nearly put to death in Japan for predicting the absolute defeat of his own nation during World War II.

> "Thousands of Americans read of my prediction of Kennedy's death, yet no one came forward to me to learn how to change his fate ... my motive in predicting the tragic end of nations, societies and individuals has always been to warn them to alter the course of their destiny ... but ... I am rarely asked about the means by which I

accomplish this. What is the reason for this low level of comprehension? In the Orient every one knows the meaning of *sanpaku* since time immemorial. Only the why has been forgotten... You are all more or less *sanpaku*... You must heal yourself before attending to anything else."

I took off my glasses, walked toward the bathroom mirror and took a cautious look. The Japanese prophet who had been right about Gandhi, Hitler, Japan, Kassem, Diem and Kennedy was certainly right about me. I had eyes like fried eggs. Sanpaku, all right. Plenty sanpaku. I tore out the Herald Tribune story and stuffed it in my pocket. For days afterward when I encountered friends or strangers, I could not take my eyes off their eyes. Every photo in the papers came under scrutiny. An appalling majority seemed sanpaku. Then I began wondering if other readers of the Herald Tribune were casing the whites of my eyes. I took to wearing sun glasses.

One evening I happened to be talking to one of America's great dancers, Carmen de Lavallade. Dancers, like athletes, are ever mindful of their physical equipment. Their bodies take continual abuse and are in need of constant repairs. They are forever changing diets, crowding the health shops, looking for magicians to repair strained backs and aching muscles with massage and all kinds of therapy. Carmen mentioned the story in the Herald Tribune. The gypsies had been talking about it. I looked at her gorgeous dark eyes.

"But *you're* not sanpaku." I suggested.

"Maybe not, honey," she laughed. "But the shape I'm in, I'm ready to try *anything*." Carmen had once slid down a metal staircase backstage in a Broadway theatre and landed smack on her spine; her back had never been the same. She had tried everything. She was way ahead of me. She had already telephoned the Ohsawa Foundation on Second Avenue and made an appointment to take a class in Macrobiotic cooking the following Sunday afternoon. She promised to keep me posted.

The idea of taking classes in cookery seemed slightly forbidding. I had recoiled at the idea of taking instruction in diaper-changing and baby-handling during my days as an expectant father. This seemed like more of the same.

But Carmen kept her promise. Sunday evening after her class, she called and invited me over for tea. She had come back from Second Avenue with a sack full of macrobiotic staples — unhusked brown rice, sea salt, soy sauce, Japanese seaweed and two kinds of tea. The whole apartment reeked of some strange exotic perfume. The windows were open to the January blast and Carmen's husband, Geoffrey Holder, was storming around trying to air the place out. It turned out that the Macrobiotic tea required pre-roasting in a pan on top of the stove. The first batch had burned and Carmen had to start over. There would be a short wait for the tea. And Geoffrey — who had survived Carmen's enthusiasm for several previous regimens and would wait for her to abandon this one — served notice he wasn't having any. In sheer self-defense Carmen showed me a book she had bought on Second Avenue; a small paperbound book titled *ZEN Macrobiotics — The Art of Longevity and Rejuvenation* by G. Ohsawa. The word ZEN was in large letters, the rest of it small print. That would have been enough to throw me off, the recent beatnik vogue for *ersatz satori* being what it was. I began skimming through the book while waiting for the second batch of tea to mature. Although written in rather basic English, it had been printed in Japan, which explained its bizarre format, oodles of misspelled words, transposed lines and typographical errors. American printers trying to set a book in Japanese characters might conceivably do worse.

It seemed to me strange that the Herald Tribune had made no mention that the Japanese prophet had written any books. Carmen agreed to lend me the little volume overnight. And for the next twelve hours I never put it down. I read it. And then I read it again. No other book in my experience had ever shaken me so deeply. *WHY* I was sanpaku was a clear as handwriting on a wall. One night's exposure to the simple, utterly subversive ideas of this man called Sakurazawa Nyoiti and/or George Ohsawa and nothing is the same anymore. "Heal yourself before attending to anything else," he said.

The next day I put on my dark glasses and headed for 317 Second Avenue. The Ohsawa Foundation occupies the first floor of an old tenement in the shadow of a cluster of modern hospitals. The front is the restaurant, the rear is the kitchen. It was shortly before dinner time and all the four tables were empty. In one corner there were shelves displaying strange-looking macrobiotic staples; in another corner a small bookstall. On a bulletin board behind the door hung a loop of string holding a bunch of photostatic reproductions of a story in the Herald Tribune. Not the sanpaku story that had brought me there. Another story by the same Tom Wolfe dated August 18, 1963. Three months before Dallas, the headline was blunt and to the point.

KENNEDY TO BARDOT, TOO MUCH SANPAKU

The text comprised a lengthy interview with George Ohsawa at the Wentworth Hotel where he spread out his scrapbook full of faces: "Pictures of President Kennedy; Albert Schweitzer; Willy Brandt; Franz Joseph Strauss; the late Davey Moore, the prize-fighter; Natalie Wood; Barbara

Powers, the wife of the U-2 pilot; Brigitte Bardot; Françoise Sagan; cover girls, all sorts of people."

"Some three years ago I have seen many pictures of Nixon and Kennedy," said Mr. Ohsawa. "Kennedy is a young man but already he is sanpaku, and so I predicted he would have many difficulties in the very near future. Three years ago I predicted it."

Here he arched his eyebrows after the fashion that says, And you see?

Sanpaku refers, literally, to an eye with three white sides. "The eyes of a sanpaku person have white showing underneath the irises — such as President Kennedy's," said Mr. Ohsawa. He put his pencil on the large stretch of white underneath the iris of the Presidential orbs.

Again, what was significant about this story were the things that were missing. There was no mention of Ohsawa's book. And no specific mention of President Ngo Dinh Diem or Abdul Karim Kassem. The first two of the fatal three assassinations had become "all sorts of people." The sharpness of Ohsawa's original prediction had been blunted somewhere along the way. Still if Winchell or Drew Pearson had printed the original prediction, it would later have been trumpeted as some kind of scoop. Astrologers who had forecast less momentous events in much less explicit language had vaulted to eminence.

Actually, as I learned much later from people who attended Ohsawa's lecture that August, his pre-vision had been even more remarkable. President Kennedy's sanpaku had been mentioned in connection with other heads of state like Diem and Kassem whose assassinations were to precede his Also, the only other U. S. President singled out for the gallery of sanpakus was Abraham Lincoln. A standard feature of the Ohsawa gallery of sanpakus is also Archduke Ferdinand of Austria who was assassinated at Sarajevo, as well as one of his doubles, dressed and uniformed to resemble him in every detail except one. The Archduke was sanpaku. The double was not.

All this was eerie, fascinating, but a blind alley. How could one relate the loss of physical and spiritual balance in the late President — or in Diem or Kassem — to the events then known to have taken place in Dallas, Saigon or Iraq? President Kennedy's wartime injuries and consequent suffering had been amply chronicled. It was no secret that he was in intermittent agony for which he was under constant treatment and medication. But how did his being sanpaku, prone to accident or tragedy, fit in with the facts then available about the gruesome events in Dallas?

"Heal yourself before attending to anything else," the prophet had said. I kept a copy of the Herald Tribune reproduction and, shielded by my sun glasses, I ordered my supply of macrobiotic staples as off-handedly as I could manage, avoiding the sympathetic stare of the hearty, healthy, grey-haired woman who was minding the store.

I bought an extra copy of the book for a sick friend, rather like a teenager making his first delicate purchase at the neighborhood drugstore. Then I went home, put the rice on the fire and began to cook by the book. I roasted some tea — with the windows open. If anyone needed the drastic ten-day regimen of plain brown rice and nothing else, it was I.

My first surprise was that the rice was edible. Then, as I chewed each mouthful 50 times by the book, I began to like it. I expected it would be hell on wheels giving up coffee, sugar, soft drinks, fruit, fruit juices, desserts, meat, potatoes and tomatoes and other things, but I was determined to give it a try. I expected it would be impossible to keep my intake of liquids down to near zero. I was a compulsive drinker of coffee, tea and soft drinks — an alcoholic about virtually every liquid but alcohol. But the Ohsawa regimen had one consolation. It said nothing about giving up cigarettes, although it discussed cancer in some detail. The official U. S. Government report linking lung cancer and heart disease with cigarettes had just been made public, and it made little or no mention of food and drink. So while so many of my friends would be trying to kick the cigarette habit — again — I would be giving up restaurants.

Ohsawa's little book supplied an answer to another

existentialist riddle: Suppose one wanted to resign from American civilization — where would one send the letter? To the Internal Revenue, the New York Times, where? A macrobiotic disciple would turn in his resignation at the neighborhood supermarket, any Chock Full O'Nuts, or at Le Pavillon or 21. Like so many forgotten folk jests, the old wheeze, "It must have been something I et," seemed suddenly more timely and profound than the latest bulletins from the AMA.

Like so many people past forty, I was not exactly sick and yet I was far from being healthy. During ten years on a New York newspaper staff, I had seen friends and fellow workers my age and younger die like flies. In New York I had never been to the funeral of anyone over 50. While in rural Michigan, where I hail from, I had rarely been to the funeral of anyone under 80. All four of my grandparents lived beyond four-score. My parents were both in their seventies and very much alive. I had always been healthy until I spent almost four years in the Army during World War II, two of them in North Africa and Europe. Much of my experience with American medicine was with its caricature — U. S. Army medicine. I nearly died of pneumonia in England, I managed to catch malaria in North Africa and after I was released I had infectious mononucleosis, hepatitis, shingles and all sorts of odd fevers. After reading Ohsawa's book, it struck me once more that in my extensive experience with U. S. physicians, I could not remember a single doctor, out of dozens who treated me, who had ever shown the slightest curiosity about what I ate and drank.

In the Army, of course, this would be absurd. Diet was decreed from on high somewhere and we were, as every mother was assured, the best-fed troops in all human history. But every instinct had set my teeth on edge against Army food. After a year of it, I developed a fancy case of bleeding hemorrhoids which scared me to death. I always associated this gruesome malady with advanced age, hardly with one's twenties. Deeper down was a childhood trauma. When I was very young my mother had gone to the Mayo Clinic, after being diagnosed as having cancer. After two operations — a colostomy — she came home a semi-invalid. Expecting the worst, I submitted to rectal surgery twice. My ailment never turned out to be cancer but surgery never did anything either to relieve the hemorrhoids for more than a few weeks. I tried everything advertised in the subways and on TV, but nothing worked.

My latest malady was even more serious. I had always been plagued with headaches. Rare was the day I didn't devour two or more aspirins. Then one day the aspirin didn't work anymore. Headaches continued for ten days until I couldn't work, sleep, eat, or move. One Sunday I cracked up completely and checked into the new Veteran's Hospital in Manhattan as an emergency case. I simply couldn't stand the pain any longer. They gave me the works: a complete physical checkup which included technical devices I had never submitted to before. After all the machines had spoken, a young doctor translated them for me. I was a perfect specimen, normal in every respect. In some details, I was in a remarkable state of preservation.

But what, I stammered incredulously, would I do about the headaches?

If they didn't go away, the doctor suggested, I should come back in a week or so. I had been prepared for the worst and this was it. I couldn't make another 24 hours. So I telephoned a skilled abortionist of my acquaintance, a brilliant man with excellent medical credentials who chose never to practice orthodox medicine. He told me to come over. He questioned me thoroughly about my examination. Then he took out a huge, forbidding syringe and sprayed something very cool up my nostrils. After an hour's nap I found some relief. I knew enough about drugs to know it had been cocaine. Well, I thought, this is how junkies begin.

Then he gave me some written instructions. Absolutely no smoking. No coffee. Oatmeal with milk and sugar in the morning. Rice for lunch. Rice and boiled chicken for dinner. His diagnosis: *Postural hypotension* — slowing down of circulation. He gave me some calisthenics to do several times a day. I took his advice. I followed the regimen. Giving up both coffee and cigarettes meant it was almost impossible for me to work, but I stuck to it until I got some temporary relief. Then I would relapse and start smoking. When the headaches returned I would quit. This modified white rice diet probably softened me up for Ohsawa's simple thesis that diet is everything. The single common denominator in both unorthodox regimens was the rice. But until I read Ohsawa I thought rice was rice was rice. I had not served in the Pacific; I'd never seen a rice paddy. I had no notion what unhusked, unpolished brown rice looked like. I knew the difference between whole-wheat bread and white bread. But I never knew there was any kind of rice except the infinite varieties in Chinese restaurants, and wild rice from Minnesota, which was not rice at all.

I stayed with plain brown rice for 48 hours until something happened that the book had not prepared me for. One morning at work, I was overcome with nausea and a crashing headache, worse than the one that had sent me to the hospital; the worst I had ever had in my life. I had a deadline to meet. I tried to keep going but it was torture. This might have been the end of auto-diagnosis and self-treatment. I have discovered subsequently that some neophytes get that far, and being scared and unprepared, blame everything on the rice and go back on aspirin, steak and ice cream. But some instinct caused me to relate my symptoms to what I knew of cold-turkey cures for drug addicts. After all, heroin is nothing but a chemical. I was kicking all kinds of chemicals cold-turkey — aspirin, caffein, sodium mono-sodium glutamate and all those multisyllabic things the government forces food processors to list — in fine print — on the backs of supermarket tins. I learned later — much later — the more violent reaction you have on the third day, the sicker you were to begin with. This could only mean I had been sick, sick, sick. I spent a gruesome day, but I slept well that night and the morning after was a revelation. I felt absolutely great and brown rice tasted better than ever.

My first precise awareness that I had changed drastically came about the fifth day. It wasn't physical at all, but emotional. I came out of a grim showdown business conference thunderstruck at having, for once, conducted myself the way I had never managed before. Usually one leaves such séances thinking of all the things one might have done, lathered with nervous perspiration, wishing one could play the entire scene over. This time was a complete switch. I had been calm, cool, collected, precise, unrattled; settled things that had been hanging fire for two years. It was all over before I was aware of what had happened. There was no other way of explaining it. Five days of brown rice had made the big difference.

The next few days brought a succession of wonders. Rectal bleeding stopped cold. Pink toothbrush — pyorrhea — "fini." The texture and feel of my skin changed completely. I had gone ten days without an aspirin. I had quit perspiring.

Cold February winds didn't bother me. My hands had a completely different feel when I washed. I was waking up three to four hours earlier in the morning with energy and bounce to burn — amazed to be able to get along on four to six hours of sleep instead of eight. My shirts were too big. Then one morning while shaving I was startled to discover I had a very definite jawline which must have been buried in flesh and bloat for years. My trousers were too large in the waist. But this had happened before. The unbelievable discovery was that my slip-in shoes were giving me blisters, my feet were swimming around in them. After two weeks I weighed myself and discovered I had dropped from 193 to 173 pounds. Since I was six feet tall with a 33-inch waist to begin with, I never considered myself fat. I had lost weight before, but never so easily, so imperceptibly, evenly all over.

Then the fun began. I visited my family after not seeing them for some months and my appearance suddenly became a conversation piece. I kept a business appointment at lunch — *toujours* lunch — and we never got around to the business. My physical transformation propelled things into an unending seminar on macrobiotics. In New York restaurants, from the fanciest to the most plain, there was rarely anything on the menu I could eat. So I ate little or nothing. That could hardly ever be explained short of an hour lecture. I began to think of myself as an Ohsawa mannequin. But all this was exterior show. The real changes were total. I was suddenly conscious of what health could be. I felt a vitality, a bounce, a calm, a clarity that was new to me. In a sudden professional showdown I met a deadline in ten days instead of thirty. I was able to work around the clock, sleep a couple of hours and work some more. In terms of sheer physical energy and endurance, I discovered I could outwork youngsters half my age and enjoy being tired. It was the season for the flu, for strep throats and such, and I seemed to be immune. Even my hair which had been receding and going grey at the temples suddenly stopped falling and began coming in brown.

On my next trip to the Ohsawa Foundation on Second Avenue, the same grey-haired lady minding the store started taking my order, then she did a long double take. "Now I remember you," she exclaimed. "I didn't *recognize* you." I took off my dark glasses, we sat down for tea and a chat. After looking me over carefully, she asked me if I would fill out a case-history chart for the files. I felt like a high school graduate who just got accepted by Harvard. The lady was Irma Paule, coordinator of the New York Foundation. When she told me *her* story, mine seemed like a small miracle indeed. Now I could understand her energy, the patience with which she performed her menial chores amid constant interruptions from the telephone, her serenity, the happiness that was so contagious.

Irma examined my hands, told me my Michigan fore-bearers had been carniverous in the extreme and a few other things, all true. Delicately she refrained from referring to my orbs. I was still plenty sanpaku and probably would be for a while. She suggested a few refinements of the regimen which could be tailored to my particular sort of degeneration, gave me helpful hints on what to do when travelling. (Find an Italian restaurant and order spaghetti with white clam sauce) or when trapped in social situations. (Take a scotch neat and sip it all night). We became firm friends.

After three months, my days as a mannequin-missionary really began. When I dropped below 150 pounds I finally had to break down and get some clothes. My shirt size had shrunk from 16 to 15; my waist from 34 to 29. I went into the store in a size 42 jacket and came out in a 38. The interim wardrobe underlined the outward change. Springtime being diet-time, overweight friends of both sexes drove me berserk asking for the secret. I grew weary of explaining I was following a regimen to get healthy; the loss of weight was only incidental. Patiently I gave them directions: Go to 317 Second Avenue, get the book by Ohsawa and take it from there. Heal yourself. But my first real convert was not a New Yorker at all. One day at Kennedy Airport I ran into Sheila, a British actress I knew, who was passing through on her way back to London from South America. She was startled to see me minus almost

50 pounds. After a few weeks in the sun near the equator she had eaten her way out of half her wardrobe. She was on her way back to London to face audiences and cameras and wanted the secret of the crash diet. There was hardly time to explain anything much except the brown rice. And I had no idea whether there was an Ohsawa Foundation in London or not. It turned out there was. I airmailed the details. In about three weeks I got back a letter which I treasure. Sheila got Ohsawa's little book, started taking the cure purely to be able to get into her working clothes — her expensive gowns. She ended up amazed at the fringe benefits: nothing less than a complete physical transformation. She recited a litany of dolors that had miraculously disappeared. After extensive surgery a couple of years before, she had been put on all sort of pills. She had tossed away the medicaments, lost almost 20 pounds in less than a month. Her before-and-after pictures were more dramatic than anything in the ladies' magazines. I felt like Dr. Kildare.

Then, through sheer fluke, I had the greatest lesson of all. For many months I had been involved in hopeless marital litigation. After four court appearances in two months, and as many adjournments, I arrived for my fifth appearance with a few rice cakes in my raincoat pocket just in case the thing dragged on until after lunch. When my case was finally called, I was greeted by two Deputy Sheriffs and a warrant for my confinement for 90 days in the Civil

Jail for contempt of court. The two Irish deputies were charming. They let me eat my last two rice cakes in a taxi on the way to the pokey, dropped me off at jail, wished me well, then rushed off to the funeral of a 44-year-old colleague in the Bronx. The jail was charming, the guards were charming, the inmates were charming and everything was lovely until suppertime. The chow, by macrobiotic standards, was lethal. Potato salad with tomatoes, Bellevue white bread, coffee, canned meat and canned fruit. And it's a long, long way from May to September. I had only once gone off the regimen since the beginning. I accepted an invitation to dinner; the hostess prepared rice and fish especially for me. But the fish was sauced with tomato and lemon. I skipped the sauce but enough had permeated the fish so I had diarrhea and bled like a stuck pig the following day. I didn't need any more lessons.

Sitting out meals in a restaurant without ordering anything — this was the kind of conspicuous non-consumption I was used to. But jail is something else. My untouched supper became a conversation piece, a focus of all eyes. I tried to make the explanation simple as possible but it was not an ideal forum for Oriental medical philosophy — not at first. I was warned in the friendliest fashion that there were no medical facilities at the Civil Jail; any hint of a "hunger strike" and I would be packed off to the Bellevue Prison Ward and fed forcibly through a tube. The jest was compounded next morning when I was assigned to kitchen duty, setting tables, doling out portions of food and washing dishes for inmates and staff afterward.

The second day without food or water and I was a little wobbly but that passed. The other prisoners divided my meals among them and cheerfully made bets on what hour of what day I would pass out and be carted off to Bellevue Hospital. On the fourth day, when I was still performing all my menial tasks, there was general amazement up and down the grapevine at my endurance. No one was more amazed than I. Three evenings a week, inmates have the privilege of ordering late snacks from a neighborhood delicatessen. I knew the menu was hopeless before I looked at it. Others ordered hero sandwiches, pizzas, soft drinks of all varieties, ice cream and cookies. I tried to get some bottled spring water but the word came back it was not to be had.

The next day, instead of calling a lawyer, I called Irma at the Second Avenue store. Her reaction was like a tonic. "That's marvelous," she said with a laugh when I told her where I was. "You've been macrobiotic for almost four months, you can go without food for thirty days at least with no danger at all. Sure, you'll get a little thin, but listen, sweetie, if there's anything wrong with you there's nothing like a good fast. That will cure anything. You had a little headache the second day and felt kind of woozy? But now you're OK. I'd give anything to get locked up for a month or so. This could be the chance of a lifetime. Prayer and fasting. Just what we all need."

Irma volunteered to find some bottled water and bring down some rice cakes to have in reserve — just in case. When visiting hours arrived, Irma was there in the crush with two bottles and a sack of rice cakes. There was such a mob we only got to wave through the bars. Then red tape reared. The matron on duty inspecting parcels allowed the rice cakes but rejected the bottled water. In the ensuing dispute I ended up in the Warden's office. It was never the twain shall meet all the way. I tried to tailor my plea to fit the rules as I knew them. I told him I had circulatory problems and "my doctor" had put me on a strict diet of 90 per cent cereals and ten per cent vegetables. "We serve cereals every morning," he said. I tried to explain that the sugar puffs and pops were verboten. He felt this was an attack on the institution whose food was, nutrition wise, of Academy Award calibre. I was about to explain I could get by on rice cakes and bottled water when he began to examine the rice cakes. I changed my tack immediately and assured him the rice cakes were frivolous supplements. I called them cookies and he let them by. But on the question of bottled water he was unbending. I could have any sugared drink from the delicatessen — but bottled water would have to be taken up with higher authority. We reached a compromise. Irma had said "Ask them to boil you some water." The Warden agreed to write out an order that I was entitled to have boiled water three times a day. With that, and Irma's reserve of rice cakes, I knew I could survive.

Sunday night the order for the boiled water had not yet filtered through channels. We were served ice tea. After almost a hundred hours without liquid, I was tempted, I took some in a spoon and sipped. It burned my mouth like boiling listerine. Word of the encounter in the Warden's Office had spread by grapevine through the entire jail. From then on it was a constant seminar in Oriental medicine. In groups, the inmates took a jocular view. There was a lot of kidding, as I headed for the shower, that I looked like something out of Dachau. But after hours, when the lights were out, the fat ones and the worried ones would always come around for serious private consultations.

On the sixth day, when I was suddenly liberated, I was down to 135 pounds. My eyes were a little deep in my head, my packages of rice cakes were untouched, but I was in better shape than when I went in. I had had only one comparable experience — having been trapped behind enemy lines in Alsace for two days without food or water. For go power or staying power, the brown rice had army chow beat hands down. It made me reflect on the logistics of Asiatic jungle warfare where the primitive supply system

— pockets full of rice — continually stymied the more elaborately equipped, lavishly rationed armies of the West.

"Heal yourself before attending to anything else," Ohsawa had written. I re-read the little book again from cover to cover. It had become my bible and I felt healed at last. When I hiked over to see Irma, she was disappointed that my fasting and meditation had been so rudely interrupted. But you can't stay out of jail when you want to, or stay in either. Over a dish of "rice cream" we had a long talk. I had accumulated a few questions. I felt immensely free and profoundly grateful to everyone in the chain of happenings that had made it possible. I wondered how many people in New York had read the post-mortem in the Herald Tribune and reacted to it as I had. Irma looked glum. "Not very many" she said. "A few old ladies, Carmen and you. That's about it."

I found it hard to believe. Carmen had followed the regimen ever since and merely become more beautiful than ever. What really disturbed me is that I hadn't really been able to reach anybody personally. It was the old business of human communication. How do you lick it? Irma had an English translation of Oshawa's latest book on cancer which had been published in Paris. Two U. S. publishing houses had already turned it down. One of them happened to have an editor-in-chief I knew and respected. He was out of town when I called so we wrote a letter trying to get him to consider it again. I bought another copy of the little Zen book and sent it to another senior editor at another publishing house in the hope he would read it and get the message. To me, Ohsawa's little book was the most important book I had read in my life. If I couldn't manage to get his newest book published somewhere in the U. S. then indeed we were all hopelessly sanpaku. Meanwhile, I had to go back to work. My week in jail had raised hob with my professional schedule. Irma was grateful. I was frustrated. She promised to let me know if she got any response from Madison Avenue. Then she said, "Why don't you try an article for one of the magazines about your own experience?"

It had never occurred to me. If the Herald Tribune (with as timely and dramatic a newspeg as could be imagined — the unique prediction of three assassinations) didn't bring them in, what could I possibly do for an encore? My story of hemorrhoids and headaches, and a six-day rest cure in the county jail, seemed pale and tired. I would be embarrassed to put it on paper. I promised to think about it and I did. According to Ohsawa, there exists neither good nor evil in this world, only *Yin* and *Yang*. The bigger the front, the bigger the back, is another axiom he invokes. Illness is the doorway to health. Tragedy turns to comedy. Disasters turn out to be blessings. Well, certainly the national disaster in Dallas had been a personal boon to me. It began a chain of events which had probably saved my life. I hadn't read newspapers or magazines for months before Dallas. It is unlikely I could have been reached in any other way except through a footnote to the Kennedy tragedy which I was following in minute detail. I made a few notes. To say anything like that in print would seem in the worst possible taste. But to skip it meant my story had no beginning. I would like to have written Irma's story but she could do that far better than I. Irma was disappointed over my refusal. I was frustrated.

Then one day out of the blue, I received a letter from Felix Morrow, president of University Books, Inc. It had been forwarded all over the lot, to jail and back, and took almost ten days to reach me. It was a Saturday morning in July. His office was closed. Monday morning I had another all-day date in court. It was Monday afternoon late before I could call his office. He answered the phone himself. The secretaries had already left for the day. He had been on his way out the door after packing his briefcase to leave for Europe the next day. I had to be back in court the next morning. He would be back on August 18. I agreed to call him then. He had a project he wanted to discuss. That for the moment was that.

But on August 7, I found myself in London. A film I had been working on intermittently since February had begun shooting in Manhattan while I was in jail. I had collaborated on the script with a French director. After the usual amount of ups and downs, its production had been taken over by a European company. Now, after more than the usual amount of difficulties, shooting had been called off. New casting was decreed. Casting would require changes in the script. The French crew was returning to Paris to salvage things, or start over.

I needed a new passport photo. Just before boarding the plane I called Felix Morrow's secretary to get the names of his hotels in Paris and London, just in case. My ticket was routed through London — the only town where I knew a true believer with a macrobiotic cuisine. From the London airport I made two calls. I called my Sheila who invited me out for a dinner of pumpkin soup and brown rice. Mr. Morrow's hotel said he was out, so I left a message, certain he was in the country for the weekend like everybody else. I was wrong. Sunday morning he telephoned and we made a date for lunch at his hotel. *Toujours* lunch.

After six months I had gotten used to being skinny. I took my physical change for granted, forgetting I hadn't seen Felix since a chance encounter on the street several pounds ago. I hadn't seen Mrs. Morrow in some years. She didn't recognize me at all. Felix was startled by my appearance and wanted to know what happened.

With other people, other publishers, one has to begin at the beginning. With Felix Morrow, one can always begin with the punch line.

"Have you ever heard of a Japanese man called Sakurazawa or Ohsawa?" I asked. As usual, Felix not only knew the man and his work, he had actually met him on one of Ohsawa's previous visits to New York. When I told him my story he expressed surprise at only one point. As a publisher, he found it difficult to believe that I had managed to straighten myself out with nothing but a book.

There is an axiom, usually invoked by publishers when they get into trouble with the law: "No girl was ever ruined by a book." Felix seemed surprised to have this axiom turned on its head. I was surprised that he was surprised because I couldn't imagine it happening any other way. I returned to my fish and he returned to his steak and we talked of a multitude of other things. Suddenly he sat back in his chair and intoned: "I have a project for you." With Felix one never knows what to expect. A never leads to B but usually to Z minor. "I was terribly impressed by Ohsawa the first time I met him. I have always felt guilty because I never followed through or did anything about my meeting with him. If you will do a new translation of his book, I will publish it."

The existing English version, printed in Japan, was in need of revision and unfair to Ohsawa himself. About this there was no argument. Ohsawa had told Felix as much. There was something about the Japanese language which came across in French better than English. But my French was rusty and inadequate, I felt. Felix was firm. "You've had the experience nobody else around has had. That's the key thing. Let's go to Paris and find the head man and get an O.K.

Irma had told me Ohsawa himself was expected in New York sometime during the summer. I decided to telephone her. Ohsawa was in California, on his way to New York. He would be in Paris for one day, August, 17 and then he was off to the south of France. Felix was leaving London for Paris the next day. He would be there until August 18. I asked Irma to try to arrange a meeting with Ohsawa in Paris for Monday, August 17. She was overjoyed. When I reported back to Felix, it was Mrs. Morrow who quietly had the last word. "If you publish the book," she said to her husband, "you'll have to go on the diet."

I had to call Sheila and give her the news. "Oh, lovely," she said.

The night before I left London, I happened to catch the news on BBC TV that De Gaulle was in San Tropez to commemorate the 20th anniversary of the Allied landings in Southern France, August 15, 1944. I was so preoccupied with the rendezvous on August 17, I completely forgot this was an anniversary for me too. It caused me to dive into my personal papers in search of an ancient laissez-passer from the First French Army, with which I had served for 15 months. I thought I would stick it in my passport. There was no telling when it might come in handy in Paris to

invoke the status of an *ancien combattant.* While fishing
through cards and papers I was startled to discover a photo-
graph taken at the beach the summer before. I couldn't
explain its being there. I didn't recognize myself. I quickly
compared it with the new photo in my passport. No *wonder*
people reacted to my altered physiognomy. Last summer I
was as bloated as Oliver Hardy; this summer, slimmer than
Steve McQueen. So I stuck the photo in my passport just
for laughs. It was still there Monday morning when I
arrived at the Librarie Ohsawa on Rue Lamartine in Paris
for our rendezvous. I had had taxi trouble and was late.
Felix Morrow was standing in the street on the look-out.
Before I could apologize, he said: "Everything is all set.
Ohsawa has agreed to everything. He's very anxious to
meet you."

When we walked into the bookshop, there was a slim
Japanese clerk wrapping up packages of books and tying
them with a string. Not until Felix spoke to him in French
did I realize this was the prophet himself. I knew he was
72 and the newspapers always said he looked no more than
50, but his youthful appearance was unbelievable. Felix
explained that from the moment he lands in France he
speaks only French. There was no turning back. He took both
my hands in his. His energy was contagious. "So you're the
man who lost twenty-five kilos", he laughed. "And without
consulting me. *Formidable!*" Then he finished wrapping the

package of books, and handed me the package. With one gesture, he seemed to say: "Here is a lifetime of writing. Do your best with them. It's your turn."

Things never happen this way. I was floored. My French was rusty and inadequate. I couldn't say what I wanted to say. So I whipped out the before-and-after pictures in my passport — Oliver Hardy and Steve McQueen — and handed them to Ohsawa. He gasped, then he laughed heartily, then he started talking in Japanese to some other people in the store, showing the photos all around. Then he looked intently at the most recent picture. "Still a little sanpaku," he murmured. I nodded. He asked me to take off my glasses and hold my head back. He looked into my eyes, he grasped the lobes of my ears. Then he took my right hand, turned the palm upward in his own and dug his thumb into the flesh below my thumb. I winced with pain. "Ah hah!" he said sadly. "You still have a long way to go. You were in very bad shape. You saved yourself just in time. In another six months you will feel much better. You were in very, very bad condition." He looked at the pictures again, laughed and said, *"Formidable."* Then he asked if he could keep them. I wrote my name and the dates on the back of each photo. He tucked them carefully into his own passport case. Then he stood up, beaming, and said: "Now everything is settled, you will be my guests for lunch." This was music to my ears. I hadn't eaten for 24 hours. There were several

macrobiotic restaurants in Paris. It had been months since
I had eaten a meal in a restaurant. We started walking up
Rue Lamartine, Maitre Ohsawa, as everybody calls him,
bouncing along the street with the explosive gait of a child.
He introduced us to his Japanese colleague, Maitre Hoki,
one of the foremost yogas in Japan, whom he had brought
with him from Tokyo. Hoki spoke only Japanese and some
English he had picked up crossing the United States. Hoki
and Ohsawa spoke Japanese to each other. We spoke French
to Ohsawa and English to Hoki. Ohsawa was always the
first to spot an empty taxi in the Paris lunch hour traffic
and first to dash into the street and commandeer the driver.
In August, of course, half of Paris is closed and shuttered;
the time of *fermeture annuelle* when everybody and his
cleaning woman is on the Riviera or in Spain for vacation.
And Monday is the *jour des fournisseurs,* the weekly holiday
for stores, shops and many restaurants. After taxiing halfway
across town, the Japanese restaurant Ohsawa had chosen
turned out to be closed. All the macrobiotic restaurants
which might have been open Monday at noon had closed
today in honor of the arrival of the Maitre. We had to give
up our cab and wait in the street because other guests were
expected. The logistics got very complicated, but the Maitre
was undaunted. He got all the guests re-routed to another
Japanese restaurant in Montparnasse. We ended up being a
table of ten.

"Papa" Ohsawa took over; he conferred with the Japanese cook, he selected the table, seated everybody, supervised every detail of the meal with an eagle eye. When the raw fish was served, he demonstrated the proper choreography with his chopsticks, and the order of the sauces. When the saki arrived, he poured. When the tempura was served and I reached first for a piece of zucchini, he quickly tapped my chopstick with his own and directed me first to the *l'angoustine*. *"Premierment Yang,"* he said. *"Apres Yin."* When the rice turned out to be white rice and Felix Morrow expressed surprise that Masa Oki started digging into it, Hoki said, "There's nothing wrong with white rice except you have to eat five times as much to get the same nourishment."

Seated opposite me, next to Maitre Ohsawa, was a charming, elegant lady from Brussels, Madame L ----. When he showed her my pictures, I began tentatively to answer her questions. "Would you believe she is over seventy?" Ohsawa asked. "You should have seen her seven years ago." Gently he touched her auburn hair. "Completely white." Now she looked a vigorous 55, no more. She explained that she had been a bedridden invalid since before the War. Scores of noted medical specialists in Europe had been consulted, to no avail. She was hoping for death when, as a last resort, some friends consulted Maitre Ohsawa.

"He came up to my bed and looked at me," she recalled.

"I couldn't move. I only wanted to die. He lifted my white hair to look at the lobes of my ears. I thought it was strange when he took them between his fingers, then he gave me a big smile. 'Madame', he said 'your ear lobes are detached like a pendant. You have a basically good physical constitution. You can heal yourself.' I stopped all medicine and took nothing but brown rice for three days. Then I thought I was really going to die of the worst migraine I had ever known, accompanied by a terrible nausea. The next day it just went away. After ten days I got out of bed and walked for the first time in years. It was incredible."

This was the first time I had met anybody else who had a violent reaction on the third day. Since her "miraculous" recovery she had travelled to Japan, and to the United States where she had met Irma Paule, and now devoted most of her time to the macrobiotic cause. She had come in from Brussels for Maitre Ohsawa's lecture in Paris the next evening. Then she was heading for Camp Ohsawa — the annual summer macrobiotic conference — in a small town near Bordeaux.

"You should come down with us," Maitre Ohsawa suggested. "A few days of good French macrobiotic cuisine — under my supervision — and you could fortify yourself."

When Felix Morrow got wind of the conference, he seconded the motion. He felt it might be the ideal place to get in training for my chores.

* * * * *

It didn't take much persuading for me to scrap my schedule one more time. The opportunity to spend a few hours or days with Ohsawa loomed as the chance of a lifetime — book or no book. The trip to Bordeaux began to look like the last lap of a pre-ordained journey to the center of the calm.

The next day I spent clearing the decks and poring over the Ohsawa books. Late that night I got a telephone call that a place had been wangled for me on the same flight to Bordeux that Ohsawa was taking. We met at Orly Airport shortly after dawn. There, a handsome young Japanese in a blue Air France uniform took care of everything — tickets, baggage, inevitable red tape. As he VIP'd us to the plane, Ohsawa introduced him as his son. At Bordeaux we were met by Guy Massat, editor of the French monthly journal *Yin/Yang,* and director of the Camp located some fifty kilometers away at St. Medard de Guizeres. We were whisked away in a car with a macrobiotic driver who — under the promptings of Maitre Ohsawa — spilled out what came to be a familiar story. Once he had been the owner of a small cafe. When he was pronounced incurably ill he had healed himself by following the macrobiotic regimen.

Now he was starting life over. In conscience he could no more sell coffee by the cup, wine by the glass, or spirits by the hooker.

It was a simple but prophetic story. It is easy to start the macrobiotic way of life, deceptively easy. But then transmutation takes over, everything changes, and there is no going back — be it to selling coffee or a multitude of other things.

The Grand Hotel du Parc in St. Medard de Guizere in the Province of Gironde sounds rather imposing. Actually it was a typically ancient and crude small town inn which had been converted for the summer into Camp Ohsawa. Ground-floor rooms had been transformed into a communal dining hall and lecture room; the kitchen had been completely taken over by a small cadre of macrobiotic cooks; most of the rooms were occupied by macrobiotic disciples from Western Europe. The green tree-shaded, walled-in park at the rear of the hotel — complete with chickens, laundry, well and outdoor W.C. — was crowded with the multicolored tents and auto-trailer arrangements of pilgrims from all over Europe. The hotel bar, like the tree of the knowledge of good and evil in the Garden of Eden, remained intact and open for local business.

While the pilgrims crowded around Maitre Ohsawa to exchange greetings and pass inspection, I first noticed the children — the first macrobiotic babies I had ever seen;

all of them were trim, compact, tranquil with an unmistake-able Japanese look. I watched them carefully for two days and only once — in the middle of a lecture — did I hear a baby cry.

After lunch — a *tour de force* of macrobiotic cuisine worthy of the guest of honor — Maitre Ohsawa grabbed me and we took a long walk through the village and the neighboring countryside. I had crammed for 24 hours trying to savor all the books Ohsawa had written from five to thirty years ago. It was no surprise to find that the man himself — in his talk and in his thinking — had leapt far beyond anything yet committed to print. He was deeply engrossed in something he calls the third industrial revolu-tion. Like Lao Tse — who divided his life into four epochs — Ohsawa divides his into: (1) development of the philosophy of non-action, most difficult of all; (2) macrobiotics; (3) distribution and propaganda; and finally alchemy. He now places himself at the end of his third period and the beginning of his final epoch. Ohsawa had decided that 1964 would be the year of his last visit to the Occident for lecturing and propagandizing; from now on he would remain in Japan and devote all his time and energies to his experiments in bio-chemical transmutation.

He had been immensely impressed some years ago by the pioneering work of a French bio-chemist, L. Kervran, author of the work *Biological Transmutation.* As a result of his collision with Kervran and his work, and subsequent experiments, he had accomplished, in Tokyo in January of 1964, the first transmutation of sodium Na into potassium K under low temperature without high pressure. He had repeated the demonstration publicly in early July before a selected group of Japanese scientists and political leaders in the House of Deputies of the Japanese Diet. The ramifications of this breakthrough were infinite and served to delay his departure for California, New York and Europe on his annual pilgrimage to the West.

The implications of his achievement were dizzying. Japan, for instance, might stop all importation of potassium — an import totaling millions of tons — and, instead, export millions of tons of sodium very cheaply because of unlimited access to sea supplies. Beyond this, Ohsawa had in his pocket a chemical formula for the transmutation of readily available chemicals into iron.

American business journals have a way of describing this age as an era of alchemy, but what they usually mean is the latest in plastic leather or ersatz fabric. Nothing, it seemed to me, quite as far-reaching as the vistas which kept the 72-year-old Ohsawa bouncing as we walked through this sleepy French village.

In New York he had already been approached by one of the giant pharmaceutical cartels. They had offered him a fancy six-figures for an option on his process for the transmutation of Na into K. What should he do? Sell the process to American capitalism? Or try the impossible and keep personal control in the hands of his Japanese colleagues for what would be only a limited time?

My chemistry was even rustier than my French. I had crammed all night before, reading up on the ancient philosophy behind the art of flower arrangements, the source and cure for diseases of the kidneys, and the formula for making an ersatz coffee out of dandelion root, and here I was confronted with cosmic conundrums worthy of the Institute of Advanced Studies.

My first counsel was to sell out to the Americans and take their money. Then the Ohsawa transmutation formula would become a secret with a price tag on it — like an overlooked Rembrandt. If the simple science of macrobiotics could come to have a fancy price tag on it, it might capture the world's imagination. Instead it seemed virtually an underground movement. Ohsawa was amused at my reaction. Clearly I was two stages behind him; a neophyte at macrobiotics — having little or no knowledge of the theory of non-action — reaching for the stage of propaganda. I was far more comfortable when it came to a discussion of writers, politics and marriage. We agreed on vegetarian GBS. He urged me to re-read Edgar Snow.

Ohsawa said he was eager to visit China and find out at first hand the extent and meaning of reports of a government-sponsored revival of ancient Chinese medicine. He also wants very much to meet Mao-Tse-tung. Who doesn't? He is virtually the only inaccessible supercelebrity left.

About marriage, especially marriage in the U. S., Ohsawa seemed genuinely alarmed. He seemed unsurprised that my marriage had been a disaster. "American women are too Yang" he exclaimed with a look of stark horror. Then he asked me for the respective birthdates of myself and spouse. As he expected, they were less than three months apart, instead of the optimum six months Japanese tradition decrees.

Later that afternoon the landscape was brightened by the arrival of Masa Oki, the foremost yogi of Japan who had driven down from Paris by car. The sight of him streaking through the 17th-century streets of a small French provincial town in his elegant long black robes and his thonged sandals was enough to send any French New Wave cinema director back to the drawing board and the story conference. But the kicker came when Hoki reached into the classic folds of his traditional costume and offered me a Kool cigarette. Here was material for a cigarette television commercial, made to order for Madison Ave., harassed by charges that it is propagandizing for cancer.

Hoki sat opposite me at dinner. His elegant way of sitting at a table, perfectly erect and relaxed, was enough to make me feel like a slob. His air of detachment and calm was enough to give one a glimpse of another way of life. Suddenly, with an electric movement, he yanked a small bouquet of field flowers out of its glass vase on the table. Breaking off a leaf here, a twig there, he set them back, superbly rearranged in the most classical order of Yin/Yang balance. Nothing, but nothing, not even something as insignificant as an off-balance flower arrangement, must be allowed to intrude on the all-important ceremony of taking nourishment.

Ohsawa's lectures, that evening and the next day, were devoted in the main to the third industrial revolution. Since they are certain to be the subject of a book next year, this is hardly the place for his ideas to be mangled in advance.

An elderly French gentleman of the town stole into the lecture hall that evening and quietly took his place near the door. He was expecting, I imagine, a discourse on strange habits of eating and drinking, word of whose magic had certainly spread through the village. Instead, like me, he found himself in a wilderness of chemical formulae and bio-chemical paradoxes and he quietly excused himself.

Later in the lecture, in a review of the progress of the macrobiotic movement in the U. S., Ohsawa produced from his wallet those inevitable before-and-after pictures of mine — Oliver Hardy and Steve McQueen. They were passed around to the assembly amid gasps and gawkings. I took an awkward bow and politely begged off delivering any remarks. But it served as an instant introduction to all the pilgrims. From thenceforward I was "the American writer who lost 25 kilos."

Taken singly or as a group, the assemblage at Camp Ohsawa presented the raw material for a dozen bad novels or one great one. Two women, for instance, sat side by side at dinner. One was the wife of a U. S. State Department official. On a cruise through the Greek islands, she had developed an intestinal infection which defied treatment. Back in Washington she had lingered in a hospital for weeks, without betterment, until her teen-age son at Harvard — having heard about the Ohsawa macrobiotic theories through an interest in judo and haikido — took leave of school, went to Washington, took his mother out of the hospital, and cooked brown rice for her for ten days until she was completely cured. She had flown down from London and driven to St. Medard de Guizere in a rented car to take in the lectures of Maitre Ohsawa. Next to her was a middle-aged Jewish lady from Paris. After two years of internment by the Nazis, she had developed acute schizophrenia. She had been an inmate of a mental hospital in Paris for seventeen years. Her elder sister, having heard about the Ohsawa theories and having tried them out on herself, arranged to get the woman released from the mental institution for three weeks. She had brought her to Camp Ohsawa where she was served plain brown rice at each meal — Regimen Number 7.

After several days, she seemed as lucid and tranquil as any of the other pilgrims.

In two days at Camp Ohsawa, I must have recounted my own experiences at least fifty times, in exchange for the stories of the other pilgrims. Any one of their experiences would make a better introduction to a book on macrobiotics than my own.

But the schedule at Camp Ohsawa was not all rice, salt and lectures. It began at seven every morning, on the green grass in the park at the rear of the hotel, with an hour of haikido. Judo, karate and haikido are so in vogue in France at this moment that one of the injunctions most often invoked in French macrobiotic circles is, "Macrobiotics first, judo second." It became my shelter and my excuse for remaining a spectator. To these unaccustomed eyes, it was a droll sight indeed to see elderly grey-haired ladies in their upper sixties bowing to each other politely before proceeding to deliver one another preëmptorily on the derriere into the wet grass.

After 48 hours in another world, a rude telephone call received in the hotel bar sent me packing back to Paris. I tried to get back to the Hotel du Parc for another few days but it wasn't in the cards. I had to start cooking my own brown rice again.

Perhaps no man can be taken seriously as a prophet in his own country; perhaps an American in Paris is an exotic and unlikely exponent of Oriental medical philosophy. At any rate, without every trying to preach, and without a single set of before-and-after pictures to document my personal transmutation, I found myself in Paris, the father of a mushrooming macrobiotic family.

It all began at a table in a cafe on the Champs Elysee where I explained why I didn't drink. That evening on the telephone I had two disciples. Two grew into five; five became ten. By now I have long lost count. Everything from raging eczema to blazing arthritis has been healed within ten days. I have heard stories of lives that have been transformed through the accidental collisions with people who had collided with me — people I have never met. Friend to friend; wife to husband; husband to wife; husband to mother-in-law; mother-in-law to friend, the word has spread. The pilgrims go to the Librarie Ohsawa on Rue Lamartine where a half-dozen of Ohsawa's books are available in French. Then they visit Les Trois Epis — the tiny macrobiotic supermarket on Rue Lamartine; they stock up on macro-biotic staples and they begin, without further ado, to heal themselves.

It is so unlike New York, it has me thoroughly baffled. Perhaps Ohsawa is right; 57th Street and Fifth Avenue is the capital, the center of gravity for the sanpakus of this world.

*   *   *   *   *

In late September, 1964, when the report of Chief Justice Earl Warren's Commission was released and in early December when transcripts of the testimony of witnesses before the Commission investigating the President's assassination finally became available, I read every line of the documents as avidly as I had read the newspaper accounts months before. But this time I read them with a special point of view — from the vantage point of a former sanpaku. I ploughed through masses of detail and then took to underlining key sentences which I later pieced together:

> *Seconds later shots resounded in rapid succession. The President's hands moved to his neck. He appeared to stiffen momentarily and lurch slightly forward. A bullet had entered the base of the back of his neck ...*
>
> *President Kennedy could have survived the neck injury ... Governor Connally felt a blow on his back. The Governor had been hit by a bullet ...*
>
> *The force of the bullet's impact appeared to spin the Governor to his right, and* **Mrs. Connally pulled him down into her lap.** *Another bullet then struck President Kennedy in the rear portion of his head, causing a massive and fatal wound.* **The President fell to the left into Mrs. Kennedy's lap.**

GOVERNOR CONNALLY: *I have often wondered myself why I never had the presence of mind enough — I obviously did say something; I said "oh, no, no, no" and then I said "My God, they are going to kill us all." I don't know why I didn't say,"Get down in the car," but I didn't . . .*

MRS. KENNEDY: *. . . Then suddenly Governor Connally was yelling "Oh, no, no, no," . . . and I heard those terrible noises. You know. And my husband never made any sound. So I turned to the right. And all I remember is seeing my husband, he had this sort of quizzical look on his face, and his hand was up, it must have been his left hand. And just as I turned and looked at him, I could see a piece of his skull and I remember it was flesh colored. I remember thinking he just looked as if he had a slight headache. And I just remember seeing that. No blood or anything. And then he sort of did this (indicating) put his hand to his forehead and fell in my lap. And then I just remember falling on him and saying "Oh, no, no, no." I mean "Oh, my God, they have shot my husband" and "I love you, Jack" I remember I was shouting . . .*

The preponderance of evidence indicated that three shots were fired. The Commission concluded that one shot probably missed the Presidential limousine and its occupants, and that the three shots were fired in a time period ranging from approximately 4.8 to in excess of 7 seconds . . .

*Expert witnesses ... testified that if the second shot
missed, Oswald had between 4.8 and 5.6 seconds to
fire the three shots. If either the first or third shot
missed, Oswald had in excess of 7 seconds to fire the
three shots ...*

There had been between 4.8 and 7.8 seconds between
the first non-fatal bullet which hit the President in the neck
and the second lethal bullet which hit his skull. Everyone
in the limousine — Mrs. Connally who pulled her husband
to safety, Governor Connally, Mrs. Kennedy and the President himself — had between 4.8 and 7.8 seconds to react,
in thought, word or deed.

Suddenly the most horrifying thing about those colored
films taken by a witness was the picture of a President frozen,
motionless, unable to do anything except clutch his hand to his
neck, an immovable target.

The Commission, of course, said little to illuminate
that point beyond the general statement that "In evaluating
the films, it was kept in mind that the victim of a bullet
may not react immediately and, in some situations, according
to experts, the victim may not even know where he has
been hit, or when."

True, the reaction in time of crisis is individual. One
learns in army combat, in automobile accidents, in drown-
ings, in every physical crisis, that a few seconds can be an eternity which spells the difference between survival and doom.

This inability to react speedily, promptly, precisely, instinctively to any challenge or accident — this is the thing one learns to measure in one's Army comrades. This is the sixth and most important index to the state of health as underlined in Sakurazawa-Ohsawa's little book, an index based on ancient Oriental texts 5,000 years old. The first five indices are worth ten and twenty points each; this last and most important one counts for 30 points.

When one is sanpaku, it means one has lost this ability to react instinctively — like an animal — to danger.

Twenty years before, Navy Lieutenant (j. g.) John F. Kennedy had been able to save himself and some of his wartime shipmates on PT. Boat 109. But Lieutenant Kennedy was not sanpaku. President Kennedy was.

In the French journal *Yin/Yang,* published in Paris, I also found the complete text of Ohsawa's reaction to the gruesome fulfillment of his prediction of the President's tragic end. At home, in the first aftermath of Dallas, the right sought to implicate the left; the left sought to implicate the right. Ohsawa, on the other hand, only blamed himself and his followers, especially those in Paris who are much more numerous and established than in the United States. "We know how to prevent and cure the sanpaku condition," Ohsawa lamented "But no one was able to reach the President and help him. If a broad French cultural group had only been able to send him a message, signed by thousands of people! But in failing to do it, we have become accomplices in the Kennedy assassination. I regret this profoundly. Why didn't this happen? Why was this opportunity lost? You are too exclusive! That too is sanpaku. People who are exclusive are destined to end as tragically as President Kennedy. The more selfish one's outlook, the more violent their end!"

I remembered seeing pictures of Roy Cohn in the newspapers in New York last year when he was on trial. Never had I seen anyone more sanpaku than he. Why hadn't I tried to reach him? Why? Because I hated his guts. That meant we were both sanpaku.

When I confronted my estranged spouse in Court, the only new thing about the encounter was my suddenly noticing that she was appallingly sanpaku and had been for years. I hadn't tried to help her either. I had tried to reach a lot of people. But not her. That meant I was still sanpaku.

Publication of this book suddenly became a compelling personal necessity. I had never felt like peddling books door to door, like the Jehovah's Witnesses, but I could begin with this one.

All the happenings of past months, the strange accidents, the wild coincidences, the unexplainable encounters, all of them seemed suddenly to fall into place.

"You must heal yourself before attending to anything

else." It had taken nearly a year for me to see the light. In that year I had lost sixty-one pounds — ending up with a completely different body. I was in much better physical shape than I had been at 25. In all other respects, as humbly as I could measure them, there was no comparison.

In this context, as in so many others, the last lines of Auden's poem seemed as apropos as the first:

> "Remembering his death,
> How we choose to live
> Will decide its meaning."
>
> W. D.

Paris   1965   January

The Divine Ritual

In ancient Japan, centuries before Christ, eating and drinking were steeped in the ceremony of a traditional sacramental rite.

The kitchen and the dining area were sacred places in the home; for it was there that the basic miracle and mystery of life — the sacrifice of the vegetal kingdom for the creation of human life and thought — was re-enacted daily. No other earthly ceremony surpassed it in importance.

Through the use of fire and salt, this miraculous and mysterious transmutation of food and water into body and blood, mind and spirit, memory of the past and procreation of the future — this was the central religious ritual of Oriental civilization centuries before Christian sacraments came to symbolize another miracle of transubstantiation.

In the Orient, since the beginning of history, the grain of rice has been identified with God. The Japanese, quite naturally, deified nourishment. The goddess Toyouke, mother-symbol of the vegetable realm, became the most revered figure in the divine constellation.

Even as bread and wine were the body and blood of Christ in the Christian sacrament, so did sages of the Orient believe, centuries before, that the grain of rice represented the deity.

Prayer was always offered to the rice before it was eaten. Eating and drinking was verily a communion between God and man.

All the great religions of the Far East were founded on principles for the establishment of health and happiness here on earth — not in some other-worldly paradise after death. Consequently all the great religions of the Far East were firmly grounded in laws and commandments governing the nourishment of the body according to the strictest of dietetic principles.

If all the great religions have lost authority through the centuries, it is because they have neglected or ignored the basic biological and physiological facts of life which, in sum, add up to the laws of nature.

Without nourishment for the body, no life is possible. To eat is to create a new life for tomorrow through the sacrifice of the vegetal realm and its miraculous green plants.

If, through ignorance or through wilful pride, man makes mistakes or commits sins against the natural laws governing the order of the universe, this is literally the *original sin* symbolized in the book of Genesis.

In the Far East thousands of years ago, it was learned that not only the body's structure but even human nature can be changed by the manner in which one eats and drinks. Therefore eating and drinking were considered the most important ritual in the divine art of life — the creation of health and happiness.

But what is health? What is happiness?

In New York, London or Paris I am not at all sure anymore how these words might now be defined. But in the Far East, happiness was defined thousands of years ago by some of the wisest of wise men. All Oriental philosophy and religion consists of practical teaching directed toward the achievement of the five factors of happiness:

A capacity for joy, a long healthy life full of amusing, interesting, brilliant experiences.

Freedom from anxiety and worry about money.

The instinctive capacity for survival — avoiding accidents and illnesses that cause premature death.

A loving capacity to understand and accept the infinite order of the universe at all times, at all levels.

Innate selflessness and good manners; never to seek to become the first, lest you should become the last; but even to welcome the last so that you may become the first forever.

What is health? For centuries wise men of the Far East have evaluated the state of health according to six conditions:

(1) **Freedom from Fatigue:** Fatigue is the consequence of illness and disease. A healthy person never feels tired. A healthy man is ready, willing and able to surmount difficulties one after another, welcoming big problems and impossible situations, taking them on as an adventure, a challenge. The bigger the problem, the greater the pleasure in coping with it.

(2) **Good Appetite:** A good appetite is health itself. If one can enjoy the simplest food, with deepest gratitude to the Creator and pleasure for himself, he has a good appetite. One who finds simple brown bread or plain brown rice appetizing, has a good appetite and a healthy, strong stomach. Sexual appetite and its joyful satisfaction are equally a condition of health. A man or woman who has no sexual desires or takes no pleasure from their satisfaction is estranged from the infinite order of the universe, is violating the laws of nature and lacking an essential ingredient of health.

(3) **Sound Sleep:** If one can fall into fast profound sleep within three or four minutes after putting his head on a pillow, under any circumstances, any place, anywhere; if one can sleep soundly without talking in his sleep or

having dreams; if one can awake at any time he wishes — at a time fixed in his mind before going to bed; if one is entirely satisfied with four to six hours of sleep each night, then one's sleep is sound and healthy. If one cannot sleep this way, there is something basically wrong with the state of his health.

(4) **Good Memory:**   Memory is the compass of our life — the most important factor and basic foundation of the personality. Our capacity to remember should develop more and more with age. Without a strong, precise and correct memory, the mind and body are little more than a machine. Without good memory, good judgment is impossible and without good judgment all our physical and mental effort can be wasted. To the extent that one remembers what he sees or hears, one has good health. Any failure of memory is a sign of bad health.

(5) **Good Humor:**   A healthy man never gives way to anger; he is cheerful and pleasant under the most trying circumstances. His voice, his behavior, even his criticism convey good humor. A healthy man has admiration for all things — a grain of sand, a drop of water — and all men. One can learn much even from an enemy who is cruel and strong.

(6) **Precision in Thought and Action:**   A man who enjoys good health is able to make sound judgments swiftly

and instinctively, acting with speed and precision. Promptness is an expression of freedom. Those who are prompt, quick and precise are always prepared to meet any challenge, any emergency, any accident. They enjoy good health. They are conspicuous for their ability to establish beauty, and order all about them in their daily lives. Life, health, divinity and eternity are one. One's personal health and happiness are expressions of the order of the universe translated into the smallest details of daily life.

Of the six conditions of health, the first three are physiological; the last three psychological. In using these ancient criteria from the Orient as a guide to evaluate one's own health, award yourself ten points for each of the first three physical criteria, twenty points each for the fourth and fifth and 30 points for the final.

Anyone who can honestly award himself 40 points out of 100 in this auto-consultation is in relatively good health. One must know in his own bones — better than any diagnostician — when something is wrong. The body does not lie.

A Land of Sanpaku

"Unless we do better, two-thirds of all Americans
now living will suffer or die from cancer, heart
disease or stroke. I expect you to do something
about it."

PRESIDENT LYNDON B. JOHNSON
April 17, 1964

The Great Society of the United States of America
enjoys what is called the highest standard of living of any
nation in the world. And yet, I have still to meet an
American child — let alone an adult — anywhere in my
travels across this great country who could score more than
60 points out of 100 in the evaluation of health and happiness established centuries ago by the sages of the Far East.

In the United States, billions are spent each year in
medical research, in medical and hospital insurance, for
medication and drugs, for surgery and medical treatment,
for hospitals and sanatoriums, in the training of more

doctors and nurses. And yet half the population suffers from some form of chronic disease and only a small percentage of all its people are free from some kind of physical ailment or defect.

The stark facts presented to the President of the U. S. by his Special Commission on the Nation's Health in December of 1964 are staggering: In 1963 heart-artery disease caused 55 per cent of all U. S. deaths, and cancer 16 per cent. Strokes killed 201,000; diseases of arteries outside the brain combined with diseases of the heart to kill 793,000. Cancer killed 285,000. Many of these deaths were premature, as witness the fact that they carried off people under 65. "Every day," said the Presidential Commission, "men and women are dying who need not die. Every hour, families are being plunged into tragedy that need not happen." The Commission proposed a governmental expenditure of three billion dollars for the first five years to make "medical miracles" available to all and for research into better methods of hospital care.

Ten years ago, another Presidential Commission reported that 25 million Americans then living would die of cancer unless the mortality rate of that disease could be lowered. President Eisenhower's personal physican reported to Congress that heart disease was a "modern American epidemic" which made the United States one of the least healthy countries in the world.

Despite widespread programs to make possible early detection and diagnosis, cancer has come to be the cause of more deaths among American children than any other disease, and second only to accidents in the cause of fatalities.

The United States has more mental hospitals and sanatoriums, more psychiatrists and psychoanalysts than any country in the world; an estimated one out of every ten Americans will spend some part of his life in a mental institution.

The United States enjoys some of the most comprehensive and costly, public and private pre-natal care for expectant mothers, and yet one retarded child is born every 15 minutes. Some five and a half million Americans are mentally retarded and in five years, according to official estimates, the total census will amount to 6.4 million, more than the entire population of the city of Los Angeles.

Every year America's giant pharmaceutical industries produce new miracle drugs and yet every winter half the population suffers from common colds or some form of respiratory illness.

American culture has made a religion out of the pursuit of sexual satisfaction and happiness, and yet literature and criminal statistics in the United States reflect the same pitiable stories of people who are the slaves of abnormal sex drives.

Allergic disorders afflict an estimated 20 million Americans. Diseases of the nervous system are the lot of another 15 million. Psychoses and psychoneuroses afflict over 16 million. Arteriosclerosis and heart disease are chronic with some 10 million. Ulcers plague more than 8 million. Muscular dystrophy, tuberculosis, multiple sclerosis and cerebral palsy condemn another million. Over ten million suffer from defective vision; a like number suffer from some sort of deafness. An estimated 15 million are sterile. Over four million are chronic alcoholics; untold thousands are addicted to drugs and/or barbituates and some forty million — or one in every five persons — suffer from chronic obesity or overweight.

Every American spends an average of $300 a year for direct medication — more than the total income of heads of families in some nations. Americans spend more than $100 million each year for pills to make them sleep; more millions for pills to wake them up. Some 15 million pounds of aspirin alone are consumed each year in the U. S. Pills by the ton to alleviate constipation; to reduce weight; pills to improve the appetite; pills to cut down the appetite; pills to pep you up; pills to calm you down; pills to break the habit of taking pills.

Official American medicine has been so fragmented — there are now so many specialists in different diseases and different areas of the human body — that a patient cannot possibly find his way anymore through the multiplying maze of medical specialties and the doctors are confused and and confounded by a complexity they themselves have wrought.

Why this chaos in a country of such brilliant materialistic and technological achievement?

Of course, the United States is not alone in this regard. Much of Western civilization — over which the U. S. exerts such a profound influence — is in more or less the same state. It is merely that in the United States the contrast between material plenty and physical and spiritual malaise is sharpest of all.

The intersection of Fifth Avenue and 57th Street in New York City may be the crossroads of America in a very limited sense, as any other intersection might be. But each time I return to America I go there to stand in fascination and horror. Sometimes I can scarcely believe my own eyes as I look into the eyes of hundreds of Americans passing by each minute.

The grim statistics — official or unofficial — tell only part of the story. The eyes of the average American tell it all. The body does not lie. And the eyes — windows to the soul — lie least of all. Almost every American I have seen is more or less *sanpaku*.

In the Far East, for thousands of years, everyone has known the grim significance of that word *sanpaku*. Yet, much to my surprise, I have found that in the West, there is no equivalent word.

The Japanese word *sanpaku* translated literally means three (san) whites (paku). The sense of the word is a condition of the human eye which presents three white sides or areas around the iris. In a healthy newborn child, the lower edge of the iris — the sphere of color at the center of the eye — rests below the lower eyelid like a rising sun. The eye has two white areas on either side of the iris. In the eyes of a dead man, the iris turns up into the skull. If it is visible at all it has three white sides. *Sanpaku.* As a man becomes old or ill, as he approaches death — whether he be seven years old or seventy — the colored portion of the eye — the iris — rises to disclose white between the lower lid and the iris.

This is the condition known for thousands of years as *sanpaku.* For thousands of years, people of the Far East have been looking into each other's eyes for signs of this dread condition. Any sign of sanpaku meant that a man's entire system — physical, physiological and spiritual — was out of balance. He had committed sins against the order of the universe and he was therefore sick, unhappy, insane, what the West has come to call "accident prone." The condition of sanpaku is a warning, a sign from nature, that one's life is threatened by an early and tragic end.

If this seems far-fetched, examine the portraits of his-

torical figures and world leaders whose careers have been cut
short by untimely death — Abraham Lincoln, Adolf Hitler,
Ngo Dinh Diem, General Abdul Karim Kassem, Marie
Antoinette, Archduke Ferdinand, President John F. Kennedy.
All sanpaku!

Sanpaku does not spare the young and beautiful. Marilyn
Monroe, as all photographs reveal, was decidedly sanpaku.
Many of the exotically slender, beautiful mannequins and
models featured in the fashion magazines have the sign of
sanpaku, and would do well to be concerned with their
future welfare.

Sanpaku is a useful portent — like pain. It points to imbalance in the human system, calls for restorative measures.

Examine yourself — and your loved ones. Are you
sanpaku?

There is a remedy. It is to be found in a philosophy
and a system of restoration through food — a diet, if you
will, or a dietary treatment of ill-health — originating in the
Far East. For Occidental usage, I call it macrobiotics.

I was brought up to believe in Western medical science.
Fortunately for me, however, "incurable" illness befell me
very early in life and I was compelled to find the doorway
to health on my own. My family, like so many families in
Japan at the beginning of the 20th century, felt the full
impact of the introduction of Western ideals of technology,
medicine and religion which had begun with the advent of

Admiral Perry almost half a century before. But my mother died at the age of 39, while under the care of Western-trained doctors. Two of my sisters died before they were ten and a brother died at sixteen under the ministrations of Western medicine. The same Western doctors told me that I had an incurable case of pulmonary tuberculosis, complicated by gastric ulcers and other things; I was then sixteen — at the age when my brother had died. Abandoned by Western scientific medicine, I was forced to work out my own salvation. Modern Occidental medicine had given up hope for me, so I returned the compliment. I decided to become my own doctor and I began to study the Oriental medicine that was more than 5,000 years old, yet had been suppressed and almost abolished by the government under the influence of Western civilization. Within five years I had saved my life by following Eastern therapy. So I decided to continue my studies and research and dedicate the rest of my years to the study of the Oriental philosophy of medicine which had saved me.

There was a famous Japanese doctor by the name of Sagen Isiduka who, shortly before my time, had re-discovered and re-interpreted the theory of the Unique Principle, which goes back four to five thousand years in Oriental history. Dr. Isiduka established the medical and bio-chemical validity of the Yin/Yang principle in the light of modern biochemistry when he discovered the complimentary antagonism between sodium (NA) and potassium (K) — a rediscovery actually of a principle that plays such a basic role in all human life.

Sagen Isiduka cured hundreds of thousands of patients — poor souls condemned and abandoned as incurable by doctors with modern Occidental medical training. He was so famous in Tokyo that any letter addressed to "Dr. Anti-Doctor" was automatically delivered to him. When he died his funeral escort was more than two miles long. In time I became practically his only successor.

I began my independent study at the very roots — seeking to learn the physical, chemical and biological origin of our bodies. I put aside all psychological, philosophical and spiritual questions until later. Putting first things first, I began with the theory and practice of nutrition. The first principles of nutrition are axiomatic.

1. He who eats, exists. He who eats can think, speak, act, love, hate, quarrel, marry, procreate, kill.
2. He who does not eat can do nothing and must, of necessity, disappear.

It follows, then, that food should be the primary concern of even the most spiritual of mankind. Without food, no Christ or Buddha. Eating is being. Like other beings, man is a transformation of foods. But what foods?

I found first that all foods have a vegetal origin. The

animal cannot exist without the vegetal. The human body cannot digest inorganic substances. The human body cannot manufacture proteins, carbohydrates, fats or minerals from inorganic substances. This synthesis of inorganic elements is a vegetal function. This process — called autotrophism — is a phenomenon the vegetable kingdom best performs. Vegetables absorb inorganic elements and convert them into organic foods, a miracle of composition and creation produced by the interworking forces of nature, and one that no laboratory has been able to duplicate. To eat meat is to duplicate a process — first in the animal, then in man.

The vegetable kingdom works ceaselessly to produce the leaves, grains, tubers, and fruits which feed the animals. The vegetable is mother to the animal. These leaves, grains, tubers and fruits are transformed into animal matter by the process of digestion and assimilation.

Who can walk under the green foliage of a deep forest without a sensation of security and peace, like a child sheltered and caressed by its mother?

Man is the prince of animals. All other animals were created to serve or amuse him. Each serves its purpose. But what reason has he, except for his sheer sensual pleasure, to feed on their flesh?

Ecologically speaking, we are all children of the vegetal mother. Without vegetable life, no animal on earth could survive. We are utterly dependent directly or indirectly upon vegetable products. Our hemoglobin is derived from chlorophyl. All vegetal foods are virgin material for the maintenance and construction of our bodies. The flesh of animals and their by-products are not. Vegetables are the superior food. We must eat vegetables or their direct products. This is a firm biological principle and fundamental natural law.

Before God said "increase and multiply" in the Book of Genesis, he said: "I give the green plants for food."

People of the Orient, especially the Chinese and Japanese, were vegetarians for thousands of years. Traditional Japanese vegetarian dishes are delicious, aesthetic, strengthening and revitalizing. They have their origin in the two great books of Far Eastern medicine: the *Charak-Samhita,* part one, and the *Ni King,* canon of Emperor Houana. These great books are the alpha and omega of Oriental medical philosophy.

After years of research and experience I am convinced that man must be faithful to the natural law and depend simply and entirely on the great vegetal mother.

If, for reasons of climate or economics, we are compelled in an emergency to eat animal foods, they are to be used only in small quantities and with special caution in their preparation and cooking to de-animalize them as much as possible.

Anatomically speaking, as witness the nature of his

teeth and intestines, man is meant to be a vegetarian. Vegetables are his normal, logical and natural food. The use of animal flesh and animal products is speculative and hazardous.

But simple vegetarianism, without the guidance of the philosophy of the Unique Principle, does not suffice either, and can descend into mere sentimentalism. Apart from the nature of his diet, man is greedy and eats too much. That is why prayer and fasting — eating and drinking simply, and being permanently aware of the order of the universe — are the gateway to health and happiness.

The first two canons of universal logic of the Unique Principle proclaim:

Everything that begins, ends.
Everything that has a front, has a back.

These two laws are the backbone of all great religions and the foundation of the Oriental philosophy of medicine.

Beginning is opposite to and antagonistic to ending, yet one cannot exist without the other. In this relative material world, the front is antithetical and opposite to the back. Birth leads to death. Happiness leads to sadness. Beauty leads to ugliness. Activity leads to weariness. Strength leads to weakness. Everything comes to an end which is the opposite of its beginning. Everything is supported, animated, maintained and destroyed by its opposite. This is the great law of nature which I call the Order of the Universe. It is the very simple yet profound law which rules our life in this relative world, as distinguished from the world that is absolute, infinite and eternal.

Once we understand this, we have no difficulty understanding or curing our so-called incurable illnesses. Without such understanding, any fundamental cure of the simplest malady will be impossible.

If one dies prematurely, because of illness or accident, it means he has lost the saving graces of the human state by having violated the Order of the Universe for many years. The tolerance of the Infinite is not boundless and limitless, but it forgives us almost to the very end. If any illness is sent to us, it is meant as a warning, an alarm signal. Illness is not sent to us as a punishment, but as a final offering of saving grace. We have only to pay heed to our bodies to know what we must do.

Instead, too many people ignore the divine alarm signal, and in the name of scientific medicine turn their bodies over to allopathically-trained physicians who endeavor to stop the pain — to kill and destroy the delicate telephonic alarm signal — through recourse to drugs or drastic surgery.

I have two quarrels with Occidental medicine. First, I find it devoid of morality and spirituality, willing to develop — at any cost — methods and medicaments that destroy only the symptoms of illness. Second, I find that Occidental medications, the miracle drugs that arrest certain disease symptoms of one generation, often create more serious illnesses and diseases in future generations.

Socialized medicine in Great Britain suddenly showered great quantities of vitamins and drugs on people who had previously not been exposed to them; some interesting discoveries were made as a result. Excess of Vitamin D taken during pregnancy was discovered to be the cause of the birth of pitifully malformed and retarded children. More recently, some widely prescribed anti-histamine drugs recommended to counteract nausea and morning sickness in pregnant mothers have caused malformations in animals. This is again the pitiful end result of blind faith in symptomatic medicine, visited most tragically on the unborn.

The medicine of the Far East — based on natural principles some five thousand years old — does not attack the symptoms of disease, but applies itself to the origin of the illness.

In the Far East thousands of years ago, medicine evolved from symptomatic medicine to prophylactic medicine, then to the yoga or religious art of health. Next it evolved into macrobiotics, or the science of rejuvenation and longevity, and finally it evolved into social medicine. The medicine of society or public health finally merged with true philosophical medicine, was absorbed and became part of the cosmological conceptions of the Universe — the Vedas, Hinduism, Brahmanism, Jainism, Buddhism, Shintoism, Christianity, Islamism and ultimately the teachings of Lao Tse.

The essential aim of all great religions has been to lead man to beatitude — infinite freedom, absolute justice and eternal happiness — by means of the practical philosophical teachings of the Unique Principle.

Disciples of modern symptomatic medicine — which is medicine in its most rudimentary and elementary form — who approach the investigation of Chinese, Indian, Japanese or Arab medicine from their limited point of view, find themselves in a labyrinth of herbs and snake cures. For modern symptomatic medicine is directed merely at curing the symptoms of disease at any cost, whether the techniques used be brutal, egocentric or immoral. It has little to offer toward curing the basic causes of illness in the patient himself.

All in all, there are seven levels of medicine which may be briefly summarized as follows:

1. Symptomatic medicine: Palliative treatment to remove symptoms.

2. Prophylactic or preventive medicine.

3. Art of Health: The study of the ways and means of acquiring and maintaining physical health.

4. Macrobiotic medicine — the art of rejuvenation and longevity.

5. Socio-moral and educational medicine aims at the

establishment of public health, freedom, and justice in society at large.

6. Philosophical medicine is directed to the mental plane of thought and judgment.

7. Supreme medicine. It is educational, biological and physiological. Its aim is to make every man his own doctor, to permit the sick person to discover all by himself the cosmological-conception of the Universe as mirrored in his own body. It not only cures diseases of the present and future, but establishes a positive state of health and happiness.

To find the medicine that cures basically and deeply, once and forever, one must attain the Seventh or Supreme Stage of medicine. One must be least satisfied with the symptomatic stage. Europeans and Americans seek the truth, it seems to me, in a maze of details by means of analytical techniques. They center too much attention on the minute microscopic examination of dissected peripheral tissue, performed by corps of specialists, rather than on the broader inquiry, looking into the eyes, examining the ear lobes, the lips, the palms of the hand, the fingers, formation of the body, posture, general appearance and performance of the whole man. The truth is whole.

Supreme Medicine — the seventh and highest stage of medicine — is exceedingly simple in its techniques but deep in its philosophical foundation. It does not attack symptoms, but applies itself to the origins of disease. Beyond that, since the ultimate cause of every illness is violation of the order of the universe through ignorance or through arrogance, Supreme Medicine is naturally inclined toward the patient and sometimes lengthy techniques of philosophy and education, rather than the quick cure by injection or amputation. It teaches man how to release his own innate instincts for survival, his own innate ability to achieve sound judgments. Disease and illness in the philosophy of Zen Buddhism prepare and dispose man to receive the perfect health and happiness that only Supreme Medicine has to offer.

Faith and Medicine

A great many authors, especially religious ones, assert that disease can be cured by faith. In a sense — but only in a sense — this is true.

Dr. Alexis Carrel, author of that revealing volume, *Man the Unknown,* was wholly convinced that, among the believers in the miracles of Lourdes who made pilgrimage there, many were actually cured by their faith.

There are in the structures and functions of the human body many marvels that modern medicine cannot account for — among these this capacity of the body to be cured of its diseases by faith. Even those who have faith, who insist upon its importance and superiority over all other therapy, cannot themselves explain the process. But the pilot who does not know the mechanism of his plane, how and why it operates, is not to be trusted.

Faith — as it is interpreted — has cured some, perhaps, but injured others. That is because it is blind faith, primitive and superstitious, unguided and often misdirected.

True faith — as it is preached by the religions of the Far East — insists upon understanding, *is* understanding of the Unique Principle (divine justice) that governs the universe. Faith is knowledge; without knowledge there can be no true faith. It is significant that many who pray for a miracle to cure them also resort to conventional medicines and orthodox Western physicians.

Even macrobiotic medicine, for all of its own miraculous cures, cannot lead to perfect health and happiness unless its Yang/Yin basis is understood and its principles adopted — in which case you can indeed be your own doctor.

Western medicine operates as blindly as "faith." Its practitioners are unable to explain the pharmacological or physical phenomena of their so-called cures. Why does adrenalin change the cardiac movement? Why has arsenic (a deadly poison) been considered a specific for certain diseases since Hippocrates? Why and by what process does aspirin lower fever? What is cardiac automatism? What is the mechanism of sanguine sedimentation, which physicians frequently rely on in their physical examination of patients? How does the antagonism between the two vegetal systems of the orthosympathetic and the parasympathetic work? What is the process of the antagonistic phenomenon they promote in the heart and stomach?

There are hundreds of such questions that cannot be

answered by analytical medicine. Is modern empirical medicine actually a modern superstition?

At its best, orthodox allopathic medicine, which relies on poisons for direct and immediate effects, is only blind fumbling, without a compass. How shall we ever know how many patients are killed as well as cured by modern allopathic medicine? How many of the so-called cures were really nature asserting itself in the interest of man against his enemies?

Understanding of how the Universe is truly constituted, the Unique Principle, the Kingdom of Heaven and its justice, the universal love that embraces all antagonisms so fully as to make them complementary — that is true faith, bringing infinite and eternal happiness to everyone.

Since it involves a lifetime of discipline, of contemplation, I cannot in this book do more than point the way.

Regrettably, the principle of philosophic medicine has all but disappeared in the Far East, where it was born.

One often fails to appreciate one's own culture. Many conveniences and inventions which Americans take for granted are the cause of awed wonder in other parts of the world. So it is in my country, too. For example, the Japanese woodblock print had no special value in Japan. It was intended mainly for the edification of the very young until the Goncourt Brothers and Professor Fenollosa, visitors from another world, found in them great artistic values. Similarly, judo, and the art of flower arrangement, were lightly considered in Japan until they were hailed as superlative arts by Western observers.

It is my hope that the Western world will view with fresh vision another gift from the Orient — in return for the many wonderful things it has given the East. I refer to our supreme ancestral treasure, more than 5,000 years old — the Unique Principle, the practical philosophy of Yin/Yang.

All things, according to this philosophy, are divided into two categories — which are at the same time antagonistic and unifying — Yin and Yang. Yin may be called the centrifugal, Yang the centripetal force.

Yin and Yang are at the same time in opposition and complimentary to each other, like day and night, man and woman, winter and summer. They are fundamental opposites that unite to destroy and unite to create everything that exists in the universe.

They cannot be totally opposite because they are always limited and relative. They blend into each other like night and day. And when it is night in the Occident it is day in the Orient. Nothing exists that is totally Yin or totally Yang — it is either more Yin than Yang, or more Yang than Yin, and so we designate them one or the other.

This "dualism" is not foreign to Western religions. Jesus realized and admitted that Satan existed even in Him, the Son of God.

According to the Unique Principle, there exists in this world nothing that is totally good or evil, just as nothing is totally Yin or Yang. In this world of relativity Yin inevitably changes into Yang, and Yang into Yin.

Only that which is eternal, absolute and infinite can be called 'good,' in the absolute sense.

On earth we call 'good' what we like, and 'evil' what we do not like — what we conceive to be helpful to *man*, and what we conceive to be harmful. What is good for one man, however, may be bad for another. Virtues, under certain circumstances, may appear as vices — as when thrift becomes stinginess; courage rashness, patience lethargy.

In this world, change is the only constant.

For those who understand the practical paradox of Yin/Yang thinking, life is a constant education in the greatest university of all, with free tuition and no fees. For those who know nothing of Yin and Yang, life can be hell.

Centripetal Yang is constrictive and produces heat, sound, density, heaviness — the tendency to go downward.

Centrifugal Yin is expansive and produces cold, silence, dilation, expansion, lightness, the tendency to go upward.

From the physical point of view, anything which contains more water than solids — every other condition being equal — is Yin; the reverse is Yang.

In terms of chemical composition, compounds rich in hydrogen, carbon, lithium, arsenic, sodium are more Yang than those which lack these elements and are rich in other elements such as potassium, sulphur, phosphorus, oxygen and nitrogen.

Everything that exists in the universe has a shape, a color and characteristic weight. A lengthened form extending in a vertical direction is Yin. The same form extended horizontally is Yang. The first is dominated by centrifugal force or Yin. The second is under the influence of centripetal force or Yang.

A B C D are vertical forms ruled by centrifugal force.

E F G H are horizontal forms ruled by centripetal force.

Each pair of forms has the same dimension, the same geometrical surface. But they are antagonistic. One is Yin, the other Yang. The antagonism between C and G, and that between D and H, are very pronounced. C and G superimposed combine to form a Judaic star of David. D and H superimposed combine to make a cross. The unification of basic Yin/Yang shapes are at root sacred symbols.

WEIGHT

Centripetal force governs anything which is heavy, therefore is Yang. Centrifugal force dominates anything

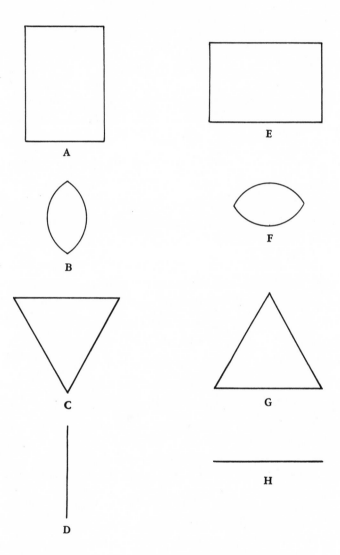

light and therefore is Yin. The lighter the weight, the more the Yin.

COLOR

Our very first sensory perception is that of color. Without color we can see nothing. The classification of basic colors is easy. Warm colors and cold colors represent the extremes of Yang and Yin — with all other degrees of warmth and coldness ranged between them. It is as simple as a rainbow ranging from the Yang extreme of red through orange, yellow, green, blue, indigo to the Yin extreme of violet.

From these three fundamental characteristics — shape, weight and color — everything in the universe can be classified as either Yin or Yang without recourse to complicated instruments or chemical analysis. This classification can be confirmed "scientifically" by reference to the Potassium/Sodium — K/Na — ratio as outlined in analytical tables. But even this later method is not exact, for the K/Na ratio can differ considerably between various specimens of the same plant, for instance, or between various parts of the same plant.

GEOGRAPHICAL VARIABLES

All things that are produced or grown in a cold climate are Yang as compared with those which adapt themselves better in warm climate. For example, a red apple from Canada is Yang. A purple mango from Trinidad is Yin. People who live in a cold climate are always stronger physiologically than those who live in a warm climate since they eat more Yang foods which are produced paradoxically more easily in cold Yin weather.

TASTE

Just as the extremes of color range from Yin to Yang, so we can distinguish Yin from Yang by taste as well as odor. The gradations from Yin to Yang are as follows: hot and pungent, sour, sweet, salty, bitter. The pimento dilates our capillaries and increases our blood flow to give a sensation of warmth. It is extremely Yin. Watercress is bitter and gives a sensation of coolness. It is extremely Yang. Remember, these tests apply only to natural tastes, not to artificial flavors or those chemically created. The sweetness of chemically produced white sugar is a hundred times that of a natural sweet taste. Chemically treated white sugar takes its place on the extreme Yin end of the qualitative scale.

Generally speaking, the most Yin vegetables are eggplants, figs, "red" raisins and "red" cabbage — both of which are really violet — the germ of the potato, oranges — particularly if they are violet inside — and sugar from the cane or beet. All of them are bluish or violet in color, inside or outside. All are rich in vitamin K and C. All are very Yin.

Yang foods, on the contrary, are red or yellow: meat and all the products of hemoglobin, fish, eggs, vitamin D, the pumpkin, carrot, yam, the apple, cherry, strawberry. They are rich in sodium (Na) in comparison to potassium (K).

The essential factor in the proper nourishment of the human body is the proper proportion of Yin and Yang.

Potassium or K may be considered as the symbol of Yin elements in our food. And sodium or Na may be considered as the symbol of Yang. The K/Na ratio is very practical as a guide since both K and Na are found in almost all chemical compositions and are the most important chemical indicators of Yin and Yang.

The best proportion of Yin/Yang or K/Na is five to one. Natural unpolished brown rice is the perfect food because it contains in itself the perfect balance of five to one. All those foods whose K/Na ratio is greater than five to one are Yin. For example, the banana is 850/1, the orange is 570/1, the potato is 512/1 and the grape fruit is 390.6/1.

Man's food has evolved with him in the seven biological stages that marked his emergence from the sea. Cereals are the final stage in this alimentary evolution, containing all the properties needed for life in its highest form — the perfect food for man.

In Japan today, according to official statistics, the most dangerous profession is not steeple-chasing, mountain climbing or even sky-diving, but medicine. Physicians as a class die at an earlier age than any other professional group. Next in order come restaurateurs. Interesting, is it not, that those who are supposed to be the guardians of our health and those who prepare delicious, tempting food for us, are not only strangers to the secret of long life, but apparently its adversaries?

On the other hand, according to official statistics, those who live longest as a group are the Buddhist monks. The traditional ways of eating and drinking, which still survive intact in Zen Buddhist monasteries, continue to confound the scientific seekers after long life and eternal youth.

In Zen Buddhist monasteries, the most superior disciples are always selected for the singular honor of becoming cooks. Theirs is the most important position in the spiritual life of the community. They are selected so that their superior knowledge and experience in the selection and preparation of food, according to the teachings of the Unique Principle of Yin/Yang, may support and sustain the developing judgment of the other disciples.

In Zen Buddhist monasteries this traditional manner of selecting, preparing and serving food is called Syozin Ryori.

The closest translation would be: "cooking which improves the supreme judgment."

The application of Oriental philosophy to the biological and physiological science of nutrition may also be translated by use of a word derived from the Greek: Macrobiotics. In Greek *macro* means great, *bio* means vitality, and *biotics* means the techniques of rejuvenation. So the word *macrobiotics* — derived from the Greeks, a people who also knew that a sound mind cannot exist in a tense and disturbed body — is used here to convey the idea of this ancient art of selecting, and preparing food so as to produce longevity and rejuvenation.

In practice, the macrobiotic way of life is very simple. It is open to everyone, rich or poor, clever or ignorant. Anyone can adapt it to his daily life anytime, anywhere. Millions of people in the Far East lived this way for centuries, enjoying happiness and freedom, culture and peace for thousands of years, thanks to the macrobiotic teachings of Lao Tse, Song-Tse, Confucious, Buddha, Mahavira, Marajuna and many Shintoists — and long before them the sages who produced the great medical science of India.

Nowadays, despite all the books written on the subject of Oriental philosophy, the most basic part of their teachings has become obsolete. All intellectual and conceptual understanding of Far Eastern philosophy is entirely futile if one cannot begin to realize a healthier, happier life for himself, beginning tomorrow morning.

If man is the prince of the animal kingdom, he should be able to cure his illnesses and safeguard his health more effectively than other animals. A man who cannot cure his aches and pains, realize his own freedom, and achieve joy and justice for and by himself, is doomed to be exploited by others, or to feed germs and microbes. He has no need to fear Hell after death for he already lives there.

All great enduring religions have one thing in common: laws and principles to guide men in eating and drinking. Some of the oldest commandments — ancient India's Code of Manu, for example — outline in great detail the most amazingly practical physiological and biological rules for the establishment of happiness and health. It is this forgotten wisdom to which we must return with gratitude and humility.

If one really says *yes* to life, and accepts the order of the universe, he can strengthen his understanding, free his judgment and decision-making capacity from their bondage to the senses by returning to natural, normal and proper nourishment.

The Cause

For every ill deed of the past we suffer the consequences
For sloth, for avarice, gluttony,
Neglect of the Word of God.

T. S. ELIOT
Four Quartets

What is disease?

Epictetus said: "If a man is not happy, it is his own fault."

Today, I fear, there are many unhappy people who would not agree with this ancient Greek axiom. Even if they accept it in theory, they are baffled as to the ultimate reason for their misery.

Let me put it another way: If a man is not happy, it means he has — consciously or unconsciously — violated the laws of nature. Through faulty judgment or sheer perversity, he has set himself and his way of life in conflict with the order of the infinite universe.

Today in the West, one rarely hears an invocation of
the "natural law" except in an argument over methods of
birth control. The Book of Genesis is invoked, with its divine
injunction, "increase and multiply." But abiding by natural
law involves more than the control of the sexual appetites.
A prior divine injunction in the Book of Genesis specifies
what man should and should not eat. And gluttony is still a
capital sin in the Christian religion, although today one rarely
hears great religious leaders preaching sermons against it.

Gluttony is a wilful estrangement from nature and
its laws. Its consequences are misery, illness and general
malaise. The sins of our fathers are indeed visited upon us,
for gluttony is often the result of embryological, familial and
social environment. But no Supreme, Omniscient, Infinite
God condemns us to it. Man is born in a state of grace —
meant to be happy on earth. All unhappiness, illness, disease and crime result from his blindness or his ignorance
of the nature of the world he lives in, or his wilful pride in
setting himself against it. Disease is a divine warning, a
message from nature seeking to guide us to the correct path.
It is, in itself, merely a symptom of deeper malady — a departure from the constitution of man as God intended him to
be. Disease can be useful, forcing man back to an understanding of the fundamental principles of health and the
inexorable laws of nature. It may temporarily injure the part
but ultimately benefit the whole — providing we recognize

and acknowledge the wholeness of the problem of health.

If we treat disease through symptomatic medicine, we are merely forestalling inevitable disaster. The operation was a success but the patient died. Chemical medication, pills, even surgical operations, serve only to blind us to the real gateway back to health. An illness so "cured" will repeat itself, or will re-emerge in another form. For, essentially, there is only one basic disease — original sin, a flouting of the laws of nature, a denial of truth through sheer ignorance or sheer perversity, a setting up of oneself against the unchanging primordial order of the Universe.

I am convinced that the notion of "incurable disease" is a human invention — the most arrogant invention of all — assigning divine responsibility for man's own failings and ineptitudes. I am certain in my own heart that there are no diseases in the world — paralysis, diabetes, leprosy, epilepsy, cancer, asthma — that could not be eliminated if we learned to apply correctly the medical philosophy outlined for us by certain of our ancestors.

I am, myself, dedicated to certain theories of healing peculiar to the Far East, and to Zen Buddhism in particular; theories that are bound up with a whole philosophical outlook, theories based on the principles of Yin and Yang, which I shall try to outline later.

In the main, this medical philosophy of the Far East has for its basis a recognition of the fact that nature — on which all life depends — is the greatest healer. And the first step towards cure, is the acknowledgment that we, ourselves, have created the disease from which we suffer. Not the bacillus, not the virus, but we, ourselves, are the guilty ones, who permitted the enemy to invade and allowed it to flourish within our bodies. *Mea culpa,* mine the guilt, are the first words spoken by the sinner who comes to the Roman Catholic confessional for absolution, and they should be the first thought of the sick man who seeks to get well.

The second step is to understand the simple wonders of the human body. Logically, all illness and disease are fed by the bloodstream. The human blood decomposes and is renewed every day at the rate of 300 million globules per second — or one-tenth of the total amount each day. Consequently, if one returns to a normal, natural and proper biological and eco-biological way of eating and drinking, the blood should be entirely transformed and renewed in ten days. Therefore, according to the constitution of the Universe as understood and interpreted by the ancient philosophy of Oriental medicine, any disease should logically be arrested, if not cured, in ten days.

All the great religions of the world, and all the great religious books of the world — including the New Testament — recommend prayer and fasting as the great healers.

If we cannot heal ourselves by prayer and fasting it means that our conception of prayer and our conception of fasting have been corrupted. Jesus cured every malady by faith. Faith is nothing but everlasting prayer. But prayer in this sense must not be confused with supplication or begging for personal advantage. Rather it is a deep and perpetual meditation — permanent contemplation of the infinite justice and divine order of the universe.

Strangely enough, many of those who profess to preach the gospels of Jesus and many of the great Buddhists as well, are often too fat, too ill, too glutted with food and drink, too sanpaku, to preach in good conscience the simple gospel of fasting and prayer. They are often the first to swallow medicaments and pills by the bottle, and they rush, at the first sign of ill health, to some hospital or clinic to be cured by the latest techniques of modern symptomatic medicine or drastic surgery, without ever pronouncing the *mea culpa* which is at the root of their misery.

Real "fasting" does not entail giving up eating and drinking entirely. One cannot detach oneself from air, water and light — the most wonderful syntheses of which are the cereals which form the very foundation of life. Fasting means abandonment of the habit of greed which causes us always to eat and drink to excess; fasting in the true sense means to eat and drink simply in accord with those principles which are at the core of the infinite order of the Universe. Fasting, too, is an antidote to over-eating.

The theory is simplicity itself; so is the logic. But the

technique is delicate and can be very complicated. Still, no theory is of use without a practical technique. And no technique is safe unless we understand the simple, clear theory it is based upon. Here is our simple theory: natural foods in proper balance, no medicine.

To be sure, as a practical matter, nothing is quite so difficult as finding natural food and drink today—especially in one of the great metropolitan centers of Western civilization where the kitchens, the markets, the agriculture and the system of food distribution are so immensely industrialized and complicated. But if you are determined to understand the unique principle at the root of the Oriental philosophy of medicine, nothing can daunt you.

We believe that if proper food can sustain health, or prevent illness, which no one denies, it can by the same token cure illness. That is, if it is introduced into the body in proper doses, which is to say in moderation, and with due regard to its chemical properties — as you would say in the West — or in terms of Yin and Yang, as we would have it in the Far East.

Food can be a medicine. It can also be a poison. But no medicine (no chemical combination) can be a food, and all medicines are poisons.

There is an area, in medical philosophy, in which East meets West. The most ardent advocate of "miracle drugs" will not deny their inadequacies, and certainly not their dangers. Bacilli develop immunity against certain drugs; the miracle drugs of one generation are found to be not only useless but often harmful to the next. Need we cite the recent world-wide scandal that ensued when it was discovered that a certain drug designed to ease the labors of pregnant women was responsible for the birth of children without hands or feet?

As for the therapeutic value of food, it is common practice in modern medicine, even in the scientific West, to deprive patients of certain foods — allowable when they are in good health — and conversely to place them on special diets, designed to restore them to health.

There is, then, some agreement that foods have therapeutic value, and that drugs are dangerous. Where we, of the Eastern tradition, differ sharply from Western practitioners, is in the values assigned to certain foods, and in the theories on which these values are based.

The Cure

Disease is not necessary, not God-ordained, therefore the efforts of Western medicine, no matter with what scientific zeal they are conducted, to analyze its nature and its specifics are wasteful, superfluous and often misleading. Adherence to a macrobiotic regimen would not only ward off all human ailments, but could arrest, and even cure, these ailments, no matter how seriously advanced the condition.

It is unfortunate that only one or two forms of medicine, chiefly the allopathic, are permitted in most Western countries, so that it is difficult to challenge by comparative results the symptomatic theories of medicine that rule the Western practice. Even in the Far East, regrettably, Western science has prevailed, and the ancient philosophy is maintained by only a few.

If I were free to do so, I could prescribe specifically for such ailments as heart disease, cancer, diabetes, venereal diseases, kidney trouble, and even the ailments in the area of psychiatry — schizophrenia, paranoia — with assurances of cure within an astoundingly short time. I could then recommend that the patient empty the contents of his medicine chest, dispense with his doctor, and — save in the most extreme emergency — deny himself the dubious salvation, particularly in the case of cancer, of drastic surgery.

I can only hope that the medical establishments in the West will be broadminded enough to investigate the therapeutic possibilties of macrobiotic food, and be guided by their true findings. It might result in reforms of standard practice, if not a revolutionary overthrow of all symptomatic medicine.

In the meantime, I can only feel free to suggest, for those unfortunates whom medical science has rejected as "hopeless cases" or those sick people who for one reason or another are not under medical care, that they would do well to follow the regimens that I shall list in this chapter, with the assurance that these comprise, at the very least, health-bringing foods that cannot but improve their conditions.

First of all, let me enumerate some of the diseases for which Western medicine, admittedly, has no cure. It does not pretend to do more than alleviate the pain and discomfort — and that at a price — of arthritis, through simple analgesics or the tricky use of hormones. Similarly, for diabetes, the only solution Western doctors have to offer is the artificial and temporary balancing of the body's chemistry through regular injections of a foreign substance, insulin — the value of which, as I stated earlier, has come to be questioned even by those who prescribe it. More to the point is their denial of sugar to the diabetic, in which they are forced to conform to the macrobiotic practice. (And why not a general rejection of sugar as food, as the Yin/Yang regimen demands, thus eliminating for all time and for everyone the danger of acquiring this disease? If tobacco — the harm of which has certainly not been proven — why not sugar?)

For cancer, stomach ulcers, no cure save surgery — which is to say, no cure at all. For leprosy, leukemia, epilepsy — alleviation at best. Syphilis spreads, despite all public health programs and "miracle-working" antibiotics; the cancer toll mounts, even in the young; and heart trouble is the Number One killer year after year.

Most surgery, too, is an admission of failure on the part of allopathic and homeopathic medicine alike. Surgeons are busy in their operating rooms performing sympathectomies. Already there exist blood banks, eye banks, and one can buy an artificial kidney. Soon there will be stomach, kidney and heart banks, too — and the process may not end until no part of a man's body may be his own! And, as the final irony, many American males, so jealous of their sexual prowess, are forced to take female hormones, endangering themselves and risking loss of their sexual drives, to arrest hardening of the arteries.

All disease is caused by an imbalance of Yin/Yang in the body. Traditional Far Eastern medicine — and it should be emphasized that this does not mean modern practice in the East, which is almost entirely under the influence of Western science — approaches every disease through successive phases, however, the cure naturally keeping pace with the progress of the disease. These stages are:

1. Fatigue, caused by an undisciplined, disorderly existence, obesity, shattered nerves. A lazy man is a sick man.

2. Pain and suffering not yet associated with specific disease but caused by sensual overindulgence or submission to whims and fads in food.

3. Chronic symptoms: caused by an excess of either Yang or Yin in food — again through caprice or self-indulgence in the selection of food. Examples are: headache, stomachache (constipation), diarrhea, vomiting, ulcers, and all diseases of the skin and blood.

4. Sympathicotonic or Vagatonic symptoms: the chronic illness has ascended to the autonomic nervous system.

5. Functional or structural changes in the organs themselves.

6. Psychoneurotic, emotional diseases — under which heading, schizophrenia, neurasthenia, hepatitis, Basedow's disease, cardiac dilation.

7. Spiritual disease. Some may be of sound constitution,
   and free of bodily or mental ailments, but they
   suffer none the less from the social consequences of
   arrogance and intolerance, and despite outward
   success, are without faith, hope, joy or love. Their
   end is inevitably tragic.

Diseases do not always lend themselves to rigid classification, and often some or all of these stages of disease are
interconnected. Obviously, the first three can be treated
separately through proper diet and disciplined living, and in
this area macrobiotic regimens, as few would deny, can truly
work wonders.

Where organic change has taken place, or in certain
serious nervous ailments which were a long time in the
making, the way back may be long — though results have
been achieved almost overnight in the case of the latter —
but traditional Yin/Yang medicine insists that it can effect
quick relief, and final cure of any disease under the sun,
including the so-called incurable ones.

Without making specific claims, but with the assurance
that they will serve to promote the general health and well-
being of any sick man, we shall list the following regimens,
deemed by Far Eastern medicine to be of more than ordinary
usefulness to the ailing body or mind. Unless contra-indicated
by dramatic emergency — such as, say, a ruptured appendix,
in which case one would do well to eat nothing — one would

do well to try them, with the warning that the use of drugs, whether recommended by physician or not, may disturb their delicate balance, and counteract their effects. Otherwise, they contain nothing harmful — whether used internally or externally. They comprise, at the very least, good foods and herbs, of a sustaining and healthy nature.

NO.	CEREALS	VEGS	SOUP	ANIMAL	FRUITS SALADS	DESSERT	DRINKING LIQUID
7	100%						Sparingly
6	90%	10%*					"
5	80%	20%					"
4	70%	20%	10%				"
3	60%	30%	10%				"
2	50%	30%	10%	10%			"
1	40%	30%	10%	20%			"
-1	30%	30%	10%	20%	10%		"
-2	20%	30%	10%	25%	10%	5%	"
-3	10%	30%	10%	30%	15%	5%	"

*Refined vegetables. In other regimens vegetables are not refined.

In explanation of the minus signs in this listing, they are so noted because they are slightly below the margin of absolute safety. A healthy person, who seeks variety in diet, may at some risk indulge in them, but they are not recommended. The state of his health and well-being may guide him, but few people, if any, enjoy perfect health or complete happiness. All would be better off if they confined themselves to the top regimens.

For reasons of health, rather than sentiment, a vegetable diet is urged upon everyone. Among the animal foods, fish is the least Yang, and is preferred over all others; indeed may be used by the normal person without marked harm. Fowl, providing it has been organically fed, is the least harmful of meats. Other meats should be absolutely eschewed, even by the apparently healthy — red meat in particular.

Not all vegetables may be safely eaten, even in the moderate degree suggested by the chart. Elsewhere in this book you will find this subject discussed, and preferences noted. There is also a listing, in the back of the book, of the Yin/Yang properties of various foods, animal or vegetal, in the order of their composition.

Again, it must be stressed that untreated cereals, in their natural state, contain all of the ingredients, in proper Yin/Yang proportion, necessary to sustain life and promote well-being.

Regimen Number 7 — consisting of 100 per cent cereals — is the easiest, simplest, wisest and swiftest way back to health, especially if you are *sanpaku,* if you are suffering from some chronic ailment, or if your auto-consultation in the six-item index to health revealed your health to be far below par.

Try this easiest, simplest and quickest way for ten days. And from now on keep the following points firmly in mind as a permanent guide to sane eating and drinking:

1. Do not use chemical white sugar and avoid everything sugared, especially soft drinks — including those which use sugar substitutes like saccharin, which is also very Yin.

2. Limit your intake of liquids to the minimum quantity necessary so that you never urinate more than twice in 24 hours if you are a woman, or three times if you are a man.

3. Use the least possible amount of animal products, especially if you live in a warm climate or are going to visit one. Almost all animal foods, including milk, cheese and butter are chemically treated or produced, while shellfish, fresh fish and wild game are usually free from chemicals.

4. Avoid industrial foods, all canned, bottled and processed foods, particularily those treated with colored dyestuff. Do not take any food, unless it is otherwise unavailable, which is imported from a long distance.

5. Avoid completely the most Yin vegetables—potatoes, tomatoes and eggplant — and do not eat any vegetables out of season or imported from a distance. This usually means they are artificially produced or pre-

served with chemical fertilizers and/or insecticides.

6. Avoid fruit and fruit juices.

7. Make sure your diet always includes from 60 to 70 per cent cereals and from 20 to 25 per cent well cooked or baked vegetables. With constant improvement in your health, you may move down the scale slowly and carefully, as you develop skill in the art of Yin/Yang balance, including in your diet soups, fish and salads. You can, however, continue with any regimen higher than Number 3 as long as you like without danger. But if you are *not* aware of constant improvement in your health as measured by the six standards, return to the Number 7 Regimen for a few weeks or months. Regimen Number 7 is the easiest, simplest and wisest. The other ways are more difficult because they are more complicated.

8. Avoid coffee and tea containing carcinogen dye. Japanese bancha tea and natural Chinese tea are permitted.

9. Avoid spices, vinegar, chemical seasoning — including all Japanese soya sauces and miso on the market. Season your dishes naturally with unrefined sea salt and soya sauce or miso macrobiotically prepared and/or approved by the Ohsawa Foundation in the U.S. or elsewhere. Use vegetable oil in cooking, being careful to limit the quantity to no more than two tablespoonsful per person per day.

10. You may use Chinese, Indian or French cooking or a combination of culinary techniques.

Inevitably after some Americans read the roster of foods that are to be avoided, someone always asks: "But then what *can* we eat?"

This question usually reveals the root of the questioner's illness and misfortune. It is an unwitting acknowledgement of that simple-minded sensory egotism and arrogance, that original sin which he continues to commit unconsciously every day.

He knows little of other cultures or civilizations which have developed the culinary art to the point that simple basic foods can be transformed into hundreds of different dishes.

One of the most famous restaurants in Tokyo is the "Tokyo Kaikan" which has several large public dining rooms and a hundred private rooms. There one can indulge in the finest foods of all nations — French cuisine, Italian, English, Chinese, as well as Japanese. The chief cook of this famous restaurant once declared, in a public lecture, his conviction of the culinary and physiological superiority of dishes prepared in accord with the Unique Principle. "In 'Tokyo Kaikan' we are ready and able to prepare any dish for our customers," he said, "but for myself I prefer dishes which my wife prepares, using Master Ohsawa's method."

Culinary art is the art of life. Our health, our happiness, our liberty and our judgment depend upon what happens in our kitchens.

The Chinese and Japanese were vegetarians for thousands of years. In that time they developed fantastic skills in the art of cooking vegetables. So much so that when a Japanese is confronted with what is called a vegetarian meal in the West, he is appalled at the coarseness and tastelessness of the food.

I have found good cooks to be extremely rare in the West, especially in the United States. If you are not a good cook, you will simply have to acquire the culinary art. You cannot depend on others.

The macrobiotic cuisine developed in our schools, based on the traditional culinary art of the Orient, is very delicious. But learning it will take time. In our cooking, one must be creative in terms of Yin/Yang proportion. Life is creative. To live is to create.

As you are learning, inevitably you will prepare dishes which are less than delicious. Never mind. If your dishes are not spectacularly successful, you will eat less. This may be very good for your stomach and intestines which in all likelihood are very tired. We are all gluttons by inclination, and sometimes the less we eat, the better.

As you study the theory more and more and practice it daily in your kitchen, your judgment and skill and confidence will develop until sooner or later you become a creative artist in the arrangement of Yin/Yang elements in your daily meals — the most fundamental and important art in your life.

The Daily Check-Up

Our happiness or misery in this world is the result of a multitude of daily decisions. Each decision involves our instinctive capacity for making judgments. Our physical, psychological — even spiritual — well-being depends largely on what we eat, how it is cooked, and the way we eat it.

The proportion of Yin to Yang in our daily diet should always be five to one. But unless one stays with a pure cereal diet, this proportion is very difficult to maintain in each meal every day. For during the preparation of our food, physical factors such as heat, and chemical factors such as salt and water, change the original ratio of raw foods by decomposing, evaporating, diluting, condensing and combining the individual elements. It is very important to understand Yin and Yang in theory, but since the distinctions are often difficult for beginners, and since cooking changes the ratio, there is another very easy and practical daily compass to serve as our guide.

By daily examination of one's fecal matter and urine with respect to color, shape and weight, one can tell if his diet of the previous day contained the proper balance of Yin and Yang.

If the urine is deep brown and transparent; if the fecal matter is dark brown or orange, in substantially good shape, long and buoyant, with a good odor, the diet of the day before had a proper 5:1 Yin/Yang balance. If one's urine and daily evacuations are too bright, one has eaten too much Yin.

A yellow, transparent urine, which shows sediments after standing for about ten minutes, points to more or less severe kidney trouble or disease, either because of an excess of calories or a shortage of Yang. A very diluted, transparent and copious urine indicates the probability of diabetes. Anyone who must urinate more than four times in 24 hours is already ill, probably with tired kidneys or heart disease.

Constipation, or its opposite — the need to evacuate more than twice a day — suggests more or less serious trouble. If one's fecal matter is greenish and easily oxidized—blackening—it suggests a large excess of Yin. The color should be deep orange or brown, neither disagreeable to the sight nor disagreeable in odor. A bad odor suggests improperly functioning stomach or intestines.

A truly healthy man — like the animals — should need no toilet paper.

Biologically, animals are merely converted vegetables — hemoglobin being a mutation of chlorophyl. Cereals and vegetables can provide a proper daily Yin/Yang balance in our food. Animal products cannot.

If we eat cereals and vegetables, their chlorophyl is transformed into hemoglobin. In our cellular nutrition, everything that cannot be transformed into red blood is discarded in the form or orange and yellow bowel movements or urine. Our physiological life is a process of turning chlorophyl products into red hemoglobic blood. Yang is created out of Yin. Cooking food helps immeasurably in this transmutation because cooking utilizes Yang factors, salt, fire, pressure and dehydration. The discovery of salt and the use of fire were of prime importance precisely because they represented the dawn of human civilization, differentiating man from the other animals.

This process of transforming chlorophyl into hemoglobin begins in the kitchen and functions unceasingly through the mouth and the digestive organs. Carbohydrates — the most Yang of compounds — are digested by the saliva in the mouth — the most Yin organ. Proteins — more Yin than carbohydrates but more Yang than fats — are digested by secretions produced in the stomach — an organ more Yang in location than the mouth. Oils and fats — the most Yin — are digested by the intestines — organs more Yang than the stomach.

Our physiological life is a transmutation of Yin colors into Yang colors. Our health, our happiness and our freedom depend upon this daily transmutation. This is the secret of life — bare, unadorned and beautiful.

The secret of death is the opposite — a daily diet based on any and every caprice and whim of the senses, lacking any sense of Yin/Yang balance and producing the illness, unhappiness, misery and agony that result from violating the order of the universe.

Food and Sex

If a Japanese man discovers hair on the legs of a woman, it makes his flesh crawl. Hair on a woman's arms is even more ominous — the arms being more Yin than the legs. This is a sign that the woman is afflicted with the most fatal and decadent malady of all — the loss of her sexuality. A woman with hair on her arms and legs is considered no longer a woman. She has lost her femininity.

In the Japanese language, the difference between the animal kingdom and the human race is expressed in the most basic terms. To be without hair is called *hito,* which means human. To have hair is called *kedamono,* which means animal.

The shedding of body hair represents a biological evolution of millions of years. Women, being infinitely superior to men biologically and physiologically, represent a further advance in that evolutionary process and are naturally endowed with smooth, beautiful, elegant and irresistable skin.

When *all* women develop hair on their bodies, that will signal the end of the world — a tragedy more cataclysmic than thermonuclear destruction. The erosion of sexual polarity — with women becoming more male and men becoming more female — has already become the most destructive and pernicious of all threats to the order of the Universe.

If man continues to become more feminine — losing his Yang qualities — and woman continues to become more masculine — losing her Yin qualities — the end result can be the end of the human race. What we are witnessing at this moment is merely the prelude to that tragedy.

Sexuality is the basis of all human life, the key to our existence, the universal attraction that Newton found in the stars and others found in atoms. Sexuality is the primordial order of the universe. Without sexuality, life simply cannot exist. And love is the flowering of that sexuality. To love is to live.

In Japan, on the seventh evening of the seventh month of each and every year, young girls and women who dream of love eternal attach seven colors of paper to bamboo poles. On each square of flimsy paper are painted love poems. Poles are mounted in front of every home — whether they be rich or poor — and the evening breeze carries off these Japanese poems of love through the skies hopefully all the way to the most distant stars.

The seven colors of paper connote the seven different

words which express the seven different kinds of love. These words, and the instincts behind them, do not exist in the West.

According to the Unique Principle and the order of the Universe the seven kinds of love are — as nearly as a different language can render them — blind love, sensual love, sentimental love, intellectual love, social love, ideological love and universal love.

Why is there so much sex tragedy in this world? Because three-fourths of the human race suffers from some malfunction of the sexual glands or the sexual organs. Sex education is a modern preoccupation in many Western countries, but almost everywhere this education is exclusively concerned with the transitory judgments of the senses, the sentiments or the intellect. Sex education in the West, it seems to me, completely ignores the biological, physiological and psychological education which guides us to the understanding of the seven stages of love and their place in the order of the Universe.

During recent visits to the United States and Europe, I have been besieged by people suffering desperately from all sorts of sexual maladies: homosexuals, women suffering from leucorrhea, men and women who are impotent or sterile, hermaphrodites (genuine or pseudo), people with deformation of their sexual organs, women with menstrual irregularities, frigid women, women who have lost what they call their "sex appeal," women who have become masculine, men who have become feminine — poor souls who mourn, protest, struggle, lament and bemoan their pitiable lot.

There are many specific illnesses of the glands and the sexual organs. But *all illnesses* — from a simple cold to an "incurable" cancer — take their terrible toll in erosion of the sexual powers.

In a country like the United States, where a huge majority of the people suffer from chronic illness of one kind or another, it is no wonder that sexual maladjustment is the rule, rather than the exception. No wonder there are so many broken marriages, so many divorces, so many desertions, so many illegitimate births, so much agony caused by abnormal sex practices. No wonder that Catholicism has felt obliged to prohibit divorces altogether in an attempt to hold families together at all costs.

Societies of the Far East are feminist despite all outward appearances to the contrary.

In Japan there are special Buddhist temples called *En Kiri,* which means the cutting of marital ties. Any woman can go there and obtain religious sanction for ridding herself of a cruel or unsuitable husband. Societies of the Far East are based on the biological and physiological superiority of women. The mother is the creator; the father is the destroyer. Man is the warrior, woman the peacemaker.

The United States is a great society which extolls human freedom above all else and yet four out of five people long pitifully for sexual freedom and suffer misery in their marital lives. Hardly one man out of a thousand seems to find continuing joy and happiness in married life. So many people cannot enjoy sexual love and their lives are a constant search for new kinds of compensatory sensory pleasure.

Most of the unhappiness and misery in family life stems from sexual difficulties — impotence, lack of joyous sex life, or its opposite — too much pathological sexual activity between the spouses.

No one can be truly happy unless his sexual needs are joyously satisfied in his family life. Many a great man has come to a tragic end because his wife was unbalanced sexually. What is the root cause of this continuing warfare between frigid women and tired, listless men, lacking the zest for the joyous consummation of their normal sexual desires?

Normal, moderate and natural sexual desire is a sign of good health. A healthy man and woman are meant to share sexual ecstacy once a night at least until they reach the age of sixty. Men and women who follow a macrobiotic regimen can enjoy sexual ecstacy until much later — even after the age of 80. One of the greatest Buddhist monks of Japan — Rennyo (1415-1499) — became the father of his 27th child when he was 81, three years before he died.

A healthy man is Yang — active, strong, centripetal. In pathological extremes, violent, destructive and cruel.

A healthy woman is Yin — passive, soft and centrifugal. In pathological extremes — weak, negative, exclusive, anti-social, escapist. Man and woman are opposites, antagonistic and complimentary. By nature their destiny is to play tag permanently. This is why life is so interesting, dramatic and amusing.

Unfortunately, there are too many souls who are completely out of place in this natural scheme of things. Some men are asexual on account of having inherited a Yin nature from the faulty diet of their mothers. Others acquired a Yin nature by consuming too much Yin food — sugar, fruits, commercial soft drinks, ice cream and liquor. Man should be Yang. If he is Yin he will be unhappy. However, if he is too Yang, on the other hand, he will become cruel and destructive. If his excessive Yang is unchecked, he will die young and tragically.

Women are by nature Yin. When they become too Yang by taking too much Yang food — principally animal products — they become miserable. They become masculine. They detest the sexual desires of men; they have no desire to love and be loved by men. On the contrary they are attracted to docile, obedient and feminine men, they devote themselves to animal pets, or they turn homosexual. Their life is miserable and unhappy because it violates all natural laws. At the other extreme are women who are too Yin to be loved; they flee from all sexuality and escape into permanent sadness.

Men who are too Yin are apt to be much more un-

happy than men who are too Yang. And women who are
too Yang are apt to be more unhappy than those who are
too Yin. This kind of basic abnormality makes it difficult or
impossible for them to build a happy home life. Sometimes,
however, an extremely Yin man and an extremely Yang
woman find each other and manage to be less unhappy
together than if each was alone — or living with birds, dogs
or fish.

Men and women are, of course, controlled by their
sexual hormones, but these in turn are influenced by diet.
Life is full of sexual difficulties and marital misery because
most men and women haven't the slightest idea of how to
establish their sexual health through correct eating and
drinking.

Everybody eats, but very few know *how* to eat.

They allow their eating and drinking — the basis of
their sexual health and happiness — to be based on sensory
taste, family habits, regional customs, laziness and conveni-
ence, routine, or current fads and fashions in food.

They are playing blindman's buff. They are also
stumbling in darkness when they choose their lifetime mates
on the basis of purely physical attraction, or for sentimental,
economic or intellectual reasons. If they understood the order
of the universe, the principles of Yin/Yang, and the correct
manner of eating and drinking, they might understand themselves. They might also be able to choose a wife or husband
more appropriate to their temperament. Or if they had

unfortunately chosen a partner who was not suitable, they would still know how to set about transforming the biological, physiological and psychological constitution of their partner — as well as their own — through recourse to a macrobiotic regime. If you told a member of a religious Japanese family, or a member of a Buddhist monastic order, that it is impossible to "change human nature" he would neither understand nor believe you.

Oriental tradition decreed for thousands of years that boys and girls were not to be allowed to play together or study together in the same room beyond the age of seven years. This is a very basic and clever way of strengthening the Yang nature of boys and the Yin nature of girls. In the Orient, all children begin to learn the basic philosophy of Yin/Yang as soon as they start going to school. The study of Yin and Yang is extremely practical and children learn quickly at a very tender age to apply it in every level and domain of living. Bio-ecologically, the Yin/Yang philosophy teaches us that the happiest marriages are those which bring together boys and girls who were born on the antipodes of the earth's orbit — that is to say some 180 days apart; those who come from families as different as possible are considered to possess a complimentary antagonism which makes for a happier and more successful union. These differences make for the strongest mutual attraction.

For thousands of years, people in the Orient have been

intimately acquainted with those vital secrets of nature — the thousands of foods and the manner of their preparation — which can change the individual human constitution, the intellectual tendency, the social behaviour, the sexual inclinations, and consequently the whole human destiny, as well as the nature of society.

Some of these foods are "miraculous" in their capacity to increase sexual prowess. I will not give any examples of Oriental aphrodisiacs here because, at this stage, they would surely be abused. It is far better to follow the natural macrobiotic regimen which transforms the entire constitution and personality slowly and steadily in the direction of total health and true sexual polarity.

Other foods are equally "miraculous" in their capacity to kill all sexual appetite and desire — instantly and completely. These have been traditionally used in Buddhist temples and among the very strict and orthodox religious families. Among them are *siitake* — a kind of Japanese mushroom; *kanpyo,* a dried gourd; *konnyaku,* a species of tuber. But these Japanese vegetables are no more calculated to dull or kill sexual appetites than sugar, sweets, fruit juices, ice cream, fruits imported from hot countries, sugared soft drinks, potatoes, tomatoes, eggplant and vitamin C.

Potatoes (solanum ruberosum), tomatoes (lypersicon esculentum) and eggplants (solanum melongena) were unknown in the Orient. They are all tropical plants, varieties of the nightshade, and seem to have been native to the Andes mountains and first cultivated by the Incas. They were introduced to the Spanish invaders by the Incas and carried by the Spaniards to other parts of Europe and North America. For years, of course, the tomato was considered poisonous in many lands and used merely as a decorative plant.

For thousands of years in the Orient, when women could no longer endure the cruelty, violence, or pathological sexual demands of their too-Yang husbands, they didn't consult lawyers or take them into court. Instead they quietly consulted older women in their family who contrived to change the diet of the husband by preparing different foods in ways that would render the overly-Yang husband docile or even impotent. Husbands who were ignorant of a macrobiotic cuisine never knew what was happening to them.

The strongest, healthiest man can be murdered—legally and without a trace of suspicious evidence — by feeding him a diet that is extremely Yin for a number of days or weeks. If that can happen — and I assure you it can — it is relatively easy to strengthen, to weaken, or to obliterate completely the sexual appetites and powers through the skillful selection and preparation of daily foods.

How can we reverse the epidemic of sexual malaise? How can we stop the vanishing of sexual polarity, which is creating men-women and women-men? How can we create vigorous healthy men and beautiful healthy women? This is one secret I will willingly share. Follow the macrobiotic regimen, specifically Regimen Number 7 for a number of days or weeks. The result will astonish you.

Verify it for yourself. The body does not lie. The condition of one's sexual health and happiness is one of the most intimate of secrets. No doctor can possibly tell you anything you do not know yourself about this function of your own body. On the immediate results the macrobiotic theories must stand or fall. Strict adherence to Regimen Number 7 for two or three weeks, and hair on the arms and legs of women will begin to disappear as the sexual glands gradually attain a condition of natural balance. Strict adherence to Regimen Number 7 and any man will discover, after a few weeks, vigor and prowess he might think had gone forever.

If husband and wife share the same macrobiotic cuisine — especially, Regimen Number 7 at the outset, which is the surest way of managing the balance between Yin and Yang — they will discover that any sexual abnormality that may exist, any incompatibility, will gradually disappear as their glands attain the original harmony established by the Order of the Universe — the same Order of the Universe which decrees absolutely and forever that every 28 days (four times seven) a woman loses a certain quantity of blood through menstruation. Blood is the essence of Yang and menstruation insures that a woman will always remain slightly more Yin than man.

Any woman who wants to regain her femininity as quickly as possible and redress a glandular imbalance caused by an over-abundance of Yang, should avoid all animal products, meat, butter, milk and cheese. These were never intended to nourish constitutions as delicate as those of a woman. Sometimes they have their uses but only at best as nourishment of the coarser and more savage male body.

We are what we eat and our nature is determined by the food we use to renew our bodies. Sexuality — the most basic and delicate of bodily functions—is uniquely dependent on our daily nourishment.

Only those who eat in accordance with the natural laws of the Universe will ever be happy. Misery will come to those who refuse to learn this lesson and live by it. They will be obliged to spend the rest of their days in a prison of their own creation.

Sexual abnormality is one of the symptoms of this misery, among many others. Homosexuality and hermaphroditism — real or pseudo — are on the increase in the West. Sexual abnormality is the most miserable illness of all — leaving men and women in bondage to the blindest animal or insect reflexes.

Next to his need for food, the desire for sexual satisfaction is the strongest and deepest need of mankind. Man lives as a result of his appetites; his appetite for food feeds his appetite for sexual satisfaction. Greediness and gluttony in turn produce abnormal sexual desires. The food addict inevitably becomes unbalanced sexually. He serves two prison terms — running concurrently.

Those who find the key to the order of the Universe can find themselves and infinite freedom. Others are destined to be enslaved all their lives to their physiological and sexual appetites.

If one is slave to abnormal sex drives, one is neither animal nor human. He is something in between. The homosexual and the asexual person are the most pitiable of all — and the literature of the West is littered with their monstrosities, from the Marquis de Sade down to the latest American novels.

Any sexual abnormality can be cured in time by strict adherence to the macrobiotic regime.

From the inhuman to the animal, from the animal to the human, from the human to the super-human, the road to happiness is a long one and the only practical guide is a reliance on macrobiotics, in accordance with the Unique Principle of Yin/Yang.

Prayer and Fasting

Four hundred years ago a small ship sailed through a tempest in the Indian ocean, swirling like a leaf caught in a raging torrent. In that small craft, a young man alone, feverish unto death and suffering, cried out: "Oh pain, send me more pain, oh, Lord."

He lived to preach in Nagasaki months later — St. Francis Xavier, the very first Christian to set foot in Japan. After thirty years of preaching, he died there.

It is his spirit, his absolute confidence, that delivers us from illness and catastrophe. Some call it faith. I call it comprehension of the Unique Principle, the loving acceptance of the Order of the Universe.

Ancient Oriental medicine has been colonized and rendered virtually extinct by modern Occidiental medicine, with its cornucopia of technological wonders, gadgets, instruments, and machines as dazzling as their counterparts in the industrial revolution. But Oriental medicine had also prepared the way for its own demise by forgetting and forsaking the Unique Principle. Everything that begins, ends.

As a practical matter, to illustrate this basic difference

between Occidental symptomatic medicine and the Far Eastern philosophy of medicine based on the Unique Principle, let us look at the same disease from two points of view. For instance, poliomyelitis. Virtually everyone in America is familiar, I dare say, with the recent history of the "war against polio" which received special attention as a result of President Roosevelt's affliction. It became the focus of billions of dollars in research, culminating in at least two vaccines and a Nobel prize for one of the discoverers.

And yet, who knows whether the polio virus really exists? The poliomyelitis virus is still a mystery to modern symptomatic medicine.

About poliomyelitis, Far Eastern medicine argues as follows: Since the legs and feet are the lowest part of the human body, they are to be considered the most Yang. Feet are locomotive organs, locomotion is movement, they are Yang organs. Yang can be neutralized or destroyed only by Yin factors. Therefore the basic cause of polio must be an excess of Yin.

Check on the daily diet of a polio victim. You will surely find in it an excess of Yin — too much vitamin C and K; chemical sugar, water, fruits, potatoes, tomatoes, syrups, ice creams, and sweets all out of proportion to other foods. The season for polio epidemics in the U.S. is late summer — the peak season for the consumption of an excess of Yin.

In the ancient methods of Far Eastern medicine, study of the physiognomy was utilized to detect a disposition toward certain diseases. Children most susceptible to polio have triangular or reverse triangular faces. Their predisposition to a disease such as polio had been prepared in their embryonic state, since our fundamental morphological construction is created by the food our mother ate while we were in the womb. Similarly children with flat feet are susceptible to polio — and also to epilepsy, encephalitis and heart disease. The arch in the sole of the foot must be strong enough, like a plate spring, to absorb the great shock which the entire body experiences at every step — bouncing down a staircase, for instance — if it is to protect the billions of incredibly sensitive cells in the brain.

Once this is understood, we may prevent polio and even cure it. It is especially easy to immunize oneself against it. We have only to abandon all chemical sugar, all sweets, chocolate, fruit juices and fruits — except apples, strawberries, and cherries, and to eschew coffee, spices, white bread, butter, cheese, meat, excess liquids — in a word, all such Yin substances as are not necessary to sustain life. Medications, operations, vaccinations, will no longer be needed.

For, strangely enough, all microbes and viruses disappear, or lose their virulence on a macrobiotic diet.

When, for once and for all, you are immunized, you need have no more fear of poliomyelitis.

To pursue the matter further, let us examine the different approaches of Western symptomatic medicine and Far Eastern medicine by underlining their different attitudes to another disease that has assumed plague proportions in the United States: diabetes.

No Western doctor can cure diabetes, even thirty years after the discovery of insulin. Physicians have continued to recommend insulin, condemning diabetic patients to walk with an insulin crutch for life. And yet on the 25th anniversary of the discovery of insulin, the inefficacy of insulin as a treatment or cure for diabetes was publicly admitted. In the meantime millions of diabetics have paid billions of dollars for this ineffective remedy, not only in the U.S. but in countries all over the world. And the beleagured diabetics are increasing every day. Once they begin taking insulin, they can expect to feed the pockets of doctors and pharmaceutical corporations as long as they live.

In diabetes, sugar passes into the urine. Symptomatic medicine prescribes insulin and forbids the patient to take food rich in carbohydrates. This provides relief, but it is more crutch than cure.

About diabetes Far Eastern medicine argues as follows:

According to the scale provided by the Unique Principle, sugar is the furthest element on the Yin extreme among foods. The lack of insulin in the body — which condenses sugar from a non-condensed form — is also Yin. Insulin, a constrictor, is Yang. The pancreas, a compact organ, is Yang in the physical sense. A malfunction of the Yang pancreas is Yin, causing a dilation everywhere but mainly in the cells of the Malpighian tubes. All in all, diabetes is caused by an excess of Yin factors — too much Yin food and drink. In consequence, the treatment must be Yang and the final remedy is a well balanced diet, neither too Yang or too Yin.

External Remedies*

Each time I visit the Occident I seem to hear about some new disease or malady. Or an old malady comes to have a new name. Diagnosis is difficult enough for doctors equipped with the myriad machines and techniques.

But the human body remains the same and each disease or malady is accompanied by one or more of the classic symptoms: fever, inflammation, diarrhea, dysentery, coughing, swelling, anemia and general weakness, or some kind of paralysis.

If one follows Regimen Number 7 faithfully for ten days, no specific suggestions are necessary. The symptoms should disappear. However, macrobiotics also has a roster of simple natural remedies, external and internal, which may prove helpful.

DENTIE: This is a tooth powder I concocted, using the head of eggplant, salted and dried, then burned. The ashes I called "Dentie." It is available through macrobiotic channels. I used the ancient principles of Oriental medicine to produce it, taking the most Yin part of the most Yin vegetable and using salt, heat, fire and time — all Yang — to obtain its Yang essence. All diseases of the mouth, particularly of the teeth and gums are very Yin, caused by Yin products rich

---

*A list of recipes at the end of this book will explain such Oriental and macrobiotic ingredients as are unfamiliar to the reader.

in Vitamin C and potassium. Dentie is extremely Yang. Apply it to an aching tooth and you will find instant relief. If you suffer from pyorrhea, brush your teeth and gums with Dentie — the outside only — before going to bed at night. It should be used also as a toothpaste twice a day.

TEA FOMENTATION: Roast bancha and make tea. Add to it five per cent seasalt and make a fomentation of this diluted tea and apply it to your eye. It is particularly good for sties, conjunctivitis. Apply it for ten to fifteen minutes three times a day.

RICE PLASTER: Crush raw whole unpolished rice with a little water. Apply this directly to any painful wound.

CHLOROPHYLL PLASTER: Watercress, spinach, cabbage, large leaves of any green vegetable should be crushed into a plaster and applied directly to the head to absorb fever. If you knock or bang your head, quickly take the cool leaf of a green vegetable and apply it to ease the discomfort.

SOYA BEAN PLASTER: Take a cup of soy beans and soak them in five parts of water overnight. Crush this mixture, add a little flour and apply this to forehead for fever or inflammation.

SALT FOMENTATION: Heat two or three pounds of un-refined seasalt. Put it in a cotton sack. Make a fomentation with this and apply to any painful part of your body.

GINGER HIP BATH: Crush one pound of ginger and put

it in a cotton sack. Boil this in two gallons of water. This is very good for violent dysentery. If the dysentery is not so violent, make half the quantity. Soak a towel in the solution and apply it as a hot compress on the abdomen.

CHLOROPHYLL HIP BATH: Take two or three riha or hosina — dried leaves of white Japanese radishes — and cook them in a gallon of water with a handful of salt. Cover your body warmly and add hot hiba water from time to time to keep the hip bath hot. This is helpful for all diseases of the female sex organs, the uterus and the ovaries. After the bath, take a cup of soyaban and go to bed.

SALT HIP BATH: Take the same bath without the hiba, using only unrefined seasalt.

PURE SESAME OIL: Filter pure sesame oil through cotton or gauze. Apply a single drop to your eye before going to sleep. Sometimes it is a little painful but it is good for all eye illnesses. Sesame oil is obtainable through macrobiotic channels and in most Oriental or Middle Eastern groceries. In many lands it is known as "sweet oil."

SESAME AND GINGER: Take one teaspoon of sesame oil and one teaspoon of ginger juice, mix them well and rub vigorously into the scalp; very effective against headaches and as a deterrent of dandruff and falling hair.

TOFU PLASTER: Squeeze white soya bean cheese — tofu — and add ten per cent flour. Stretch this over any painful or inflamed part of the body for immediate relief.

Internal Remedies

FOR FEVER: Drink Kuzu, Ume-Syo-Kuzu and whole rice cream. Externally apply Plaster of Chlorophyll, Tofu, Soya Bean or Carp.

FOR INFLAMMATION: Externally try plaster of Albi, Carp, Tofu or Chlorophyll following the application of the ginger fomentation.

FOR DIARRHEA OR DYSENTERY: Drink Kuzu or Ume-Syo-Kuzu. Externally try Ginger Fomentation, Konnyaku or a Ginger Hip Bath.

FOR A COLD: Kuzu, Ume-Syo-Kuzu and whole rice cream.

FOR COUGHING: Kohren tea or Lotus tea is an excellent remedy for whooping cough. Externally use ginger fomentation and Albi plaster.

FOR SWELLING: Radish (Daikon): Drink Number 2 or Aduki juice.

FOR ECZEMA OR WOUNDS: Strict observance of Regimen Number 7. Nothing else. Externally, raw rice crushed with a little water may be applied directly on painful wounds.

FOR PARALYSIS: Strict observance of Regimen Number 7, with as little drinking as possible. Watercress or dandelion minced in tiny pieces and sauted in a small amount of oil and salt, or dusted with gomasio, is sometimes very helpful.

FOR ANEMIA AND GENERAL WEAKNESS: Strict observance of Regimen Number 7, drinking very little. Also try mincing one ounce of lotus root, 1 1/2 ounces of burdock root, 1 ounce of carrot. Fry the burdock in 2 ounces of oil, then add the lotus and carrot and cook well. Then add 1/5 ounce of ginger and 5 ounces of miso. Add another 2 ounces of oil and cook until it becomes very dry. This is called Tekka Number one.

FOR PARASITES AND AMOEBIC DYSENTERY: Take a handful of raw rice in place of breakfast, chew each mouthful a hundred times. Observe Regimen Number 7 very strictly, using gomasio. Eat an umeboshi plum every other day.

The Sacred Act

For the treatment of everything from airsickness to varicose veins, for all diseases and ailments of the human body, there is one basic prescription: Prayer and fasting. In other words, rigid adherence to Regimen Number 7 and deep meditation on the absolute justice and infinite wisdom of the Order of the Universe.

The almanac of human ills which follows, together with specific symptomatic discussion, is merely an elaboration of that simple statement. There are some small variations in the use of specific secondary dietary suggestions, to the extent that the ailments proceed from too much Yin or too much Yang. You may find these useful or comforting. But the more the external or specific symptomatic remedies change, the more the ancient prescription of prayer and fasting remains the same.

AIRSICKNESS: For this malady, as well as seasickness and morning sickness, drink as little as possible before flying. No alcohol, sugar or sweets. Especially avoid the chewing gum and bonbons handed out by the stewardess. Instead, keep a little gomasio in your mouth while airborne. If you have the stamina to observe Regimen Number 7 for one or two months, you will never be sick again in the air or on the ground.

APOPLEXY: If you follow a macrobiotic regimen, you need never fear this illness. You are immune to it. For those who have been attacked by it, rigid adherence to Regimen Number 7 is advised.

APPENDICITIS: Again, no macrobiotic person can be afflicted with this disease. Regimen Number 7 is the answer for those who are its victims. The best external remedy is ginger fomentation followed by Albi plaster.

ARTHRITIS: Like other "incurable" diseases, this one is amenable to cure through strict observance of Regimen Number 7. Externally, try Ginger Fomentation and Albi plaster.

BURNS: Absolutely no water at all for a few days while observing Regimen Number 7, with an umeboshi plum added to it every other day. Sesame oil is helpful externally.

BASEDOW'S DISEASE: Very easy to clear up with Regimen Number 7 and gomasio.

CATARACT: This is caused by eating too much sugar and

Vitamin C over a long period of time. Regimen Number 7 is recommended with gomasio.

CONSTIPATION: Again, the cause of this ailment is too much Yin food and drink — sugar, vitamin C, fruits, salads, french fried potatoes, tomato sauces, and salads. Stop eating these things and you will be cured, as if awakening from a nightmare. If Regimen Number 7 does not give you complete relief in a few days, your case is extremely serious. Your intestines have lost all elasticity and are completely paralyzed. Wait a few more days, weeks even. Do not worry as long as you adhere to Regimen Number 7. No poisonous fermentation will be produced in your intestines by taking natural macrobiotic food. Don't be afraid, as long as your intestines have established their original elasticity.

COUGHS: By adhering to Regimen Number 7 with gomasio, any coughing, including whooping cough, will stop in a few days. Even a 20-year old asthmatic cough will submit to this treatment. Lotus tea and kuzu are also helpful.

MUSCULAR CRAMPS: Once more the cause is too much Yin, fruits and sweets. It usually attacks the legs which are most Yang and which can ordinarily neutralize too much Yin. If cramps attack the heart, the result can be fatal. Cramps, like other symptoms and sufferings, are God-given telegraphic alarms. If you take sedatives, drugs or symptomatic treatments, you are jamming the fire-alarm system without getting near the cause of the fire.

DANDRUFF, FALLING HAIR, BALDNESS: Too much drinking of water, too many sweets, fruits, sugar, Vitamin C — all things rich in potassium — these are the cause of all three scalp ailments. Avoid their use and you will be cured without any treatment. (When you are cured, try this interesting experiment, bearing out the cause of the ailments. Take one of the Yin foods — a tomato, a pear, some eggplant, vinegar or honey before going to bed. In the morning you will find hair on your pillow and in your comb — ten times as much as the day before.) In brushing, use natural wood-and-hair brushes. Plastic combs and brushes, cosmetics, lotions and dyes are all very Yin.

DIARRHEA AND DYSENTERY: Again, the cause is too much Vitamin C or too much fruit. Adhere to Regimen Number 7 and do not drink any water. Apply ginger fomentation and Albi plaster to the abdomen. Take a cup of Kuzu or Ume-Syo-Kuzu. For dysentery in children, the cause and treatment are the same. A ginger hip bath may be easier to administer and just as efficacious.

ECZEMA: All eczema is the result of kidney disease. No symptomatic treatment is necessary or recommended. Observe Regimen Number 7, drinking as little as possible.

EPILEPSY: Jesus cured this disease with prayer and fasting and no modern practitioner of symptomatic medicine has been able to duplicate his "miracles". The easiest way to cure epilepsy is with Regimen Number 7, drinking no liquid at all for several days. My wife has frequently cured this "incurable" malady within three days.

HEADACHES: Headaches are warnings of possible incipient cerebral hemorrhage. They are caused by too much food rich in Yin. Taking aspirin to kill the pain is suicidal because you are eclipsing your illness by paralyzing your nervous system, your radar, your self-defense warning. Headaches are God-given alarms indicating too much acidity in the blood, and aspirin is a strong acid — as are all vitamins. A headache is a signal that danger has penetrated into the very source of your life. Adhere rigidly to Regimen Number 7 and you will get relief. Take as much as a spoonful of gomasio. The following drinks are also very good: Yannoh, Kokoh, Mu Tea, Syo-Ban, Kuzu, Ume-Syo-Kuzu. Rice cream is also very effective.

HEMORRHOIDS: (Piles). Rigid adherence to Regimen Number 7. If you are suffering severely try Ginger Fomentation and Albi plaster externally.

HERNIA: Follow Regimen Number 7 strictly augmenting it with Kobu. Kobu is a wide green seaweed, available in dried form through macrobiotic channels or in Japanese stores. Take a thick kobu, wash it in water and keep the water for other cooking because it contains precious minerals. Cut the kobu into one-inch squares. Add three parts of water and cook well until it becomes dry. Add 10 to 20 per cent soy sauce and cook again until it becomes dry.

HYPERINSULISM: This is a disease of transition before the onset of hypoinsulism which is diabetes. This is easily cured by adhering to Regimen Number 7.

INFLUENZA: Whole rice cream Kuzu, Ume-Syo-Kuzu and Mu Tea are helpful additions to Regimen Number 7. It goes without saying that once you adhere to the macrobiotic regime you become immune to influenza.

IMPOTENCE: See the chapter on sexual maladjustments on Page 121.

INSOMNIA: Follow Regimen Number 7 rigorously and take a cup of soya ban — bancha tea with soy sauce — before going to bed.

JAUNDICE: Complete fasting — no food or drink for three days — is recommended. Then rice cream with a little umeboshi. If jaundice occurs in a baby fed by mother's milk and cannot be cured in a few days, it is very dangerous. The mother must make herself Yang by eating Yang food. None of this is necessary for the infant.

LEUCORRHEA: (White, green or yellow). This is very common. Women afflicted with this disease are miserable no matter how rich, beautiful or clever they are. The green variety is most Yin. Follow Regimen Number 7, augmented with hip baths, taken very hot, fifteen minutes before retiring for at least two weeks.

MIGRAINE: This can be cured easily in a few days with Regimen Number 7 and a little gomasio.

MENSTRUAL IRREGULARITIES: Regimen Number 7 with Mu Tea. Drink less water. Try one of the hip baths.

MYOPIA: Most varieties of this disease are caused by the expansion of the diameter of the eye, which is Yin. Some types of myopia, however, are caused by an increase of the refractive power of the lens, something caused by too much Yin and sometimes caused by too much Yang. Either variety can be cured by Regimen Number 7, augmented with 30 to 60 grams of raw white radish (daikon) and a little gomasio. This should be followed for a month or more.

PERIOSTITIS: Regimen Number 7 with a little gomasio. Externally, try ginger fomentation and albi plaster four times a day.

PROLAPSUS: Again Regimen Number 7 with a little gomasio. Ginger fomentation and albi plaster.

PARANOIA: Physiology being linked with psychology, it

is obvious that mental disease can be cured by dietetics. Mental disease responds well to macrobiotic treatment and cure because mental patients are often in good physical condition. Paranoia is a variety of schizophrenia which has an extreme Yin basis, along with a pathologically excessive component of Yang, leading to violence and cruelty. Regimen Number 7 is recommended with no Yang preparations of any kind.

RHEUMATISM: Drink less and less. In following Regimen Number 7, limit yourself to rice or rice cream, served as thick as possible. Again ginger fomentation and albi plaster are good externally.

SCHIZOPHRENIA: A mental illness characterized by the separation of mental and physical processes. This disturbance is a Yin illness, characterized in most forms by a lack of Yang (centripetal force) and a loss of the boundaries of self, a feeling of unreality and detachment from the world, and even detachment from one's own body. As cancer is the extreme Yin illness of people with originally strong physical constitutions, schizophrenia is the most extreme Yin illness of people with weak constitutions. Regimen Number 7 should be followed strictly for three weeks at least. Soyo-ban and other Yang drinks are also recommended.

STOMACH ACHE: Rice cream and a little gomasio. Soyo-ban and ume-syo-kuzu as drinks. Externally, ginger fomentation and albi plaster are sometimes helpful.

STERILITY: Regimen Number 7 should be followed absolutely and strictly for at least two weeks, and then Regimens Number 6 to Number 4 for many months. Either of the two hip baths, very hot, should be taken 15 minutes before going to bed.

TOOTHACHE: Apply Dentie to the aching teeth or surrounding gums. No drinking of Yin liquids.

TRACHOMA: Regimen Number 7 with a little gomasio. Whole rice cream is recommended as is Kinpura, for which the recipe is listed under Tekka. There are two kinds of Tekka. The first kind is listed under general suggestions. The second one is made by mincing two ounces of lotus root, 1/2 ounce of burdock root, 1/2 ounce of carrot, 1/5 ounce of dandelion root. Fry the burdock first in two ounces of oil, until the vegetables are very dry.

VARICOSITY: You can clear up varicose veins very quickly with Regimen Number 7, avoiding everything Yin. A fifteen-minute hip bath before going to bed is very helpful for women.

This partial almanac of diseases and remedies will give you a general idea of the macrobiotic approach to physical and mental illness, developed through experience and my

interpretation of the most ancient Oriental medical philosophy. Those who have combinations of diseases must study,
contemplate, listen to their own bodies, and treat themselves,
just as the animals do. Everyone must be and can be his
own doctor. Once you have attained insight into the practical
philosophy of the Orient, and genuine deep faith in the
absolute justice of the order of the universe, nothing shall
be impossible to you.

If you have followed Regimen Number 7 faithfully
for ten days or two weeks, you will have surely caught a
glimpse of happiness and health. That, in turn, may help
you to understand some of the statements in this book which
at first may have sounded arrogant, childish or absurd.
Following a macrobiotic regimen will help you to understand
macrobiotics better than reading a book about it. It will
help you to understand why anyone who follows a macrobiotic regime can be immunized permanently and completely from all diseases.

If you have freed yourself from illness, major or minor,
and have been able to measure the appreciable improvement
in your health resulting from observance of the ancient rules
set forth at the beginning of this book, you can be more
adventurous and try more and more complicated regimens
from Number 6 on down, adding vegetables as long as
they are locally grown and in season, such as onions, carrots,
pumpkin, radishes, cabbage, cauliflower, watercress, endive

and lettuce. Also, depending on your geography, your diet can include wonderful wild vegetables like the dandelion, coltsfoot, burdock, shepherd's purse and cress. There are thousands of edible wild plants, leaves, roots, buds, flowers, grains, seeds, produced by God without any commercial intent.

They have gone out of fashion since the frontier days of your great grandparents, and have never been harvested for sale. Therefore they are usually pure, free of fertilizers and chemicals. All of them are delicious when properly prepared, and of great medicinal value.

You will also learn how to prepare soup, to make bread, create all sorts of delicious dishes which are original with you. You may even learn how to use animal food, especially shellfish, in small quantities carefully prepared and creatively served.

All animal foods are forbidden in Buddhism, especially Zen Buddhism, as they are among many branches of the Christian Church in America, such as the Seven Day Adventists. The Roman Catholic injunction against eating meat on Fridays and on selected Ember days, during Lent and Advent, has its roots deep in ancient tradition.

Zen Buddhism which prohibits animal food entirely is the superior type of Buddhism, biologically and physiologically. Without *Syozin Ryori* — cooking which improves the supreme judgment — without macrobiotics, there is no true Buddhism.

But as you are probably in no great rush to attain *satori,* you may eat special dishes from time to time until at last you are free of any dependence on the animal kingdom.

In the meantime, it is not our desire to create a morbid fear of any and all animal foods. If you have established the proper Yin/Yang balance in your system, and exercise proper caution, you can learn to neutralize the effects of animal food. It is all a matter of degree and proportion. Quantity changes quality; Yin can become Yang. A drop of water has different properties than an ocean. Even the desirable becomes undesirable in excess. But before you experiment, you should have learned the philosophy of the Unique Principle and the practical techniques of the macrobiotic cuisine.

You may make mistakes, but also you can correct them. Your stool will give you a clue (as indicated earlier) by the shape, weight or color of your evacuations. If there is any imbalance, return at once to Regimen 7 for a period of days or weeks until you are completely in health again. You should, nevertheless always stay within the 10 regimens from Number 6 on down, through the minuses. The lower you go on the scale, however, the more complicated the balancing acts you will have to perform.

Under any circumstances, however, you should obey the

following "don'ts" — to avoid mistakes common to beginners in macrobiotic cooking.

Do not peel vegetables. Scrub them well, and learn to use every particle of each vegetable. The skins of onions, the tops of carrots, the leaves of cauliflowers. It requires only imagination and daring to use these creatively in your cuisine.

Never soak a vegetable in water, either whole or shredded. Avoid the use of too much oil in cooking. Two tablespoonsful per person per day is the maximum.

Avoid eating vegetables in too great quantities. Consider them principally as seasoning and garnish for your principal food — cereals. Your daily nourishment should be from 70 to 90 per cent cereal. Two tablespoons of cooked vegetables with each meal is a safe limit.

Avoid using too much water in preparing food. In general cereals should be well cooked, and yet dry enough to require thorough chewing. Never bolt your food, or neglect to masticate properly. If you chew each mouthful 30 to 50 times it will help to keep you from eating too much. You can eat as much cereal as you want, however, if you chew properly.

Do not go overboard on salt. One must Yangize progressively, not all of a sudden.

Do not try to limit your liquid intake too drastically in order to heal yourself, and then relapse abruptly into old drinking habits or binges. Drastic changes are a strain on the entire system.

Do not pamper yourself while following a macrobiotic regimen. Lots of exercise, plenty of good hard manual labor, the maximum physical activity are useful, if not essential to macrobiotic regimens.

Stop taking pills or medicaments of any kind.

Do not waste food — not even a grain of rice. If everyone wasted one grain of rice per meal, these three billion grains per meal would, in one year, suffice to feed one million people. Avoid cooking too much food. And do not be afraid to eat "spoiled" or "decomposed" cereals. There is no danger in their use — quite the contrary. Decomposition is digestion and it will save your stomach some labor. Rice covered with mold can be digested very easily.

After you have healed yourself with Regimen Number 7 and moved into more complicated diets, a good rule of thumb is: do not eat anything which in its living state could resist or run away. Vegetables, seaweed and shellfish are in this category.

Do not eat any industrialized food treated with chemicals. After your body has become used to normal, natural, macrobiotic food, processed industrialized food, containing many chemicals, is particularly lethal and you can expect an immediate reaction.

You may eat anything else that accords with the order of the universe — even fruit in season which is organically grown and free of chemicals. The order of the universe is absolute justice. If America produces 200 million apples a year, you should eat one apple every summer. This is justice. If you eat more, you have robbed your neighbor and you will be punished — sooner or later — by being confined to a reformatory called illness.

About Salt

The sea around us accepts all things: it welcomes the wastes of our rivers, transforming them into its own shimmering likeness, beautiful and pure. The sea's immensity embraces all fearsome things: multiplying parasites, microbes without number and viruses that wear man's enemy brand; the stinking pus, the poisoned blood, the lethal radioactive chemicals, the excrement of millions of cities and billions of men. It transforms all rotten waste into shimmering crystals of emerald green.

Cleansing everything it touches, renewing everything within reach, the sea gives life to every flora and fauna, like the mother of all life on earth, animal and vegetable. Man has his source in the sea that surrounds him. And what is the secret of the sea's power to cleanse, renew, create?

The salt of the sea.

Without salt, the sea, for all its expansiveness, would be nothing but an enormous cesspool, a breeding ground for germs and microbes. Seasalt transforms all untouchable microcosms into a spectacular netherwold of plants and living things of unearthly beauty. The sea changes everything, yet ever remains the same. Salt is the secret of its miracle. Salt is the magician. And salt is Yang.

Man's origin in the sea around him left a mark on him for all eternity; the salt in his blood. Without salt in his veins, man, like the fish out of water, gasps and dies. Man's salty bloodstream is a miniature replica and souvenir of his watery origin. Like the salt of the sea, the salt of the blood cleanses, renews, transforms all dangers into life-giving necessities, nourishing our cells, supplying us with oxygen. If the blood loses its saltiness, the consequence is sickness unto death.

If man lacks salt, evil and misery multiply. If the world around us is plagued with evil, misery, crime and conflict, it is because the followers of Christ have forsaken his commandment: You must be like the salt of the earth. And they have glutted themselves with the extracted essence of forbidden fruit.

Man created civilization after his discovery of fire and salt. Salt has been considered the most precious thing in our daily life since the dawn of history. The first roads through uncharted wastes were made by animals seeking and finding a source of salt for their survival. Men who resisted the lure of gold have been known to sell their wives and children into slavery in exchange for salt. Salt is the international standard of wealth, above and beyond gold. Even today, explorers venturing into uncharted territories carry bags of salt to present to unknown or unfriendly peoples. The word "salary" means payment in salt.

The most important and fundamental function of the human body results from a balance or equilibrium between sodium and potassium in the blood, especially the brain — the seven inches between the root of the nose and the occiput — our most prized possession.

More than thirty years ago at the Sorbonne in Paris, Professor Quinton developed the theory that all biological beings on earth originated in the sea. His work was the result of a lifetime of study. His fascinating book *L'eau de Mer* or *Sea Water* was read and accepted by scientific scholars all over the world. His laboratory in Paris and his clinic on the Atlantic are world famous. He coined the word "thalassotherapie" to signify the use of salt in therapy and his "Quinton Plasma" has been a staple element in Western medicine ever since.

Yet to the amazement of this visitor from the Extreme Orient, the fear of salt pervades Western symptomatic medicine. Salt-free diets have become vogue; salt-free products and foods have been created to exploit this phobia. I am unable to discover any foundation for such notions.

Anyone can safely take a little natural unrefined sea salt or gomasio — sea salt mixed with roasted sesame seeds — in conjunction with a macrobiotic diet. Try it for ten days or for one. You will find there is no danger at all, but instead an improvement in your condition if you take it in reasonable amounts.

Don't be taken in by the changing superstitions and fashions of symptomatic medicine. Let your own body give you the answer.

About Sugar

In relation to sugar or sucrose, on the other hand, Western medicine and science has only just begun to sound alarm signals over the fantastic increase in its per capita consumption, in the United States especially. Their researches and warnings are, I fear, many decades too late.

Chemically refined white sugar is a fairly recent development of Western civilization. Crude unrefined cane, maple and beet sugar had been a rare luxury until quite recently in the history of man. It was entirely unknown in the time of Buddha, Lao Tse and Jesus Christ, else it would have figured in the writings of the period. It is quite different from the natural fructose of vegetable and fruit sugar which contains all the minerals, proteins, oils and vitamins needed to maintain our vitality. Industrially refined sugar completely lacks these natural elements and contains many chemicals very detrimental to human health.

I am confident that Western medicine will one day admit what has been known in the Orient for years: sugar is without question the number one murderer in the history of humanity — much more lethal than opium or radioactive atomic fall-out — especially for those people who eat rice as their principal food. Sugar is the greatest evil that modern industrial civilization has visited upon the macrobiotic countries of the Far East and Africa. Sugar turns to water and CO_2 in the body, it decreases Yang elements in the blood and increases the ratio of K to Na. It is the most Yin of all products used as human food and is the direct cause of numerous fatal diseases.

Every year the giant sugar trust devises new ways of unloading the huge oversupply of industrial sugar on the hapless people of the world. And today the average American child consumes sugar at an appalling rate compared to the children of fifty years ago. Is it any wonder then that leukemia and other cancers take the lives of more innocent children every year in the United States than any other disease? Western science admits the havoc wrought on the teeth of young children by sugared drinks, candy, ice cream and pastries. The rest of the body is hardly immune. Just as spilled sugar attracts ants and insects in our kitchens, so does it attract microbes and parasites in our bodies.

Cancer is, of course, a Yin disease, characterized by the expansive multiplication of cells in one or another organ of the body. Its basic cause is always an excess of Yin in the daily diet. Cancer of the blood appears only in those who glut themselves with sugared drinks, ice cream, sugared milk, sugared coffee and tea. Interesting, is it not, that those who are greedy for the sweet things in life perish automatically?

A child reared on a macrobiotic diet who is given a lump of sugar will spit it out automatically because it burns his mouth.

Those foolish people who give or sell candy to babies will one day discover, to their horror, that they have much to answer for.

About Milk

In China, Japan and even India, people lived for thousands of years without drinking animal milk. Even today, more than a billion people of the Orient drink tea without adding sugar or milk.

Why has the West made a religion out of drinking milk? Cow's milk was intended to nourish calves. There is no reason for man to live on the milk of an animal — especially an animal inferior to him biologically and intellectually.

People of the Orient do not shun milk for sentimental reasons. They avoid it because they respect the biological natural laws of the Order of the Universe. Milk is the indispensable nourishment for calves before they have teeth. Once the young offspring of animals have their teeth and are weaned from nursing, they no longer drink milk. Cows and dogs never allow their young to nurse once they have teeth. No animal ever does.

The "milk-for-babies" as a theory of nutrition is a sentimental modern superstition commercially conceived and propagated. The mortality rate among children artificially fed with animal milk is demonstrably higher than among

169

children nourished with human milk. They may be able to improve the quality of animal milk and thus lower infant mortality, but it will never be possible to turn animal milk into human milk. This biological natural law cannot be broken. A child fed on animal milk is, literally, physiologically and biologically related to the calf. He is dull, wanting in intellect, delicacy, sociability and spirituality.

In the Orient for thousands of years, there has existed a traditional regime of biological and embryological education to be followed by women from the onset of pregnancy until the day the child no longer nurses at the breast. The sustenance of a newborn child is provided exclusively at its mother's breast. The mother's daily life, all her activities, her diet, her reading, her thoughts are strictly regulated in accord with the Unique Principle, the order of the Universe.

If a mother has no milk to give her baby, or if she dies shortly after its birth, it is the task of the family leader to find a suitable wet nurse. In the selection of a wet-nurse, everything about the substitute mother must be known: her background and that of her family and her husband's family; her personality, her physical and intellectual activities, her physical beauty, her fidelity, and above all her astrological characteristics. She must be a healthy, active, creative, intelligent and moral woman. The Far Eastern mother who cannot nurse her baby would never think of adopting a wet-nurse who did not possess all these qualities. Oriental families know that the embryological education and early nourishment of an infant are much more important than the selection of a college for his education years later.

No Oriental family would think of turning the nourishment of a child over to a wet-nurse chosen at random, any more than they would think of turning the care and nourishment of a child over to the intermittent whims of a commercial dairy industry.

The quality and quantity of a mother's milk controls her child's destiny. In cases where the mother's milk is not available, babies can be fed with *Kokoh* — a macrobiotic cereal milk made with roasted rice, glutinous rice, oatmeal, soya beans and sesame seeds reduced to powdered form.

About Liquids

Drinking less liquid is very difficult — especially in America where the simple minded "drink-as-much-as-you-can" theory has been so much in vogue for so many years and where the consuming of great quantities of chemically-produced sugared drinks has become a national addiction. It is much more difficult to drink with reason than to eat wisely and simply, but it is utterly necessary for our health and happiness.

In terms of quantity, water is the most important compound in our bodies. Seventy-five per cent of our body weight is water. But an excess of water in the system can reduce our vitality, since this means a decreased ratio of blood; it lowers our body temperature and forces the heart and kidneys to overwork.

Water is constantly evaporating since it is dominated by centrifugal force — Yin. Generally, those who are very active physically drink much more water than those who are not. They lose their body's water through activity and perspiration and become thirsty. But all other elements being equal, that which contains water is more Yin than that which is dry. Those who drink great quantities of liquid and are not very active physically become very Yin — chilly, inactive, shy, weak and lazy.

Cooked rice, for instance, contains 60 to 70 per cent water, and most vegetables contain 80 to 90 per cent water. Thus we are inevitably consuming liquid, Yin, even when we are not drinking. If one adds water to a grain of cereal that already contains 13 per cent of water, it swells, decomposes (Yin) and begins to germinate (Yin). All these activities are expanding and therefore Yin.

People are generally more placid when it rains, but much more active and happy when the weather is clear. This is especially true if one suffers from rheumatism.

Rheumatism is a Yin disease which can be cured by drinking little water and eliminating from one's diet all food that is rich in water — especially sugar which turns to water and CO_2 in the human body — decreasing the amount of Yang components in the blood and increasing the proportion of K to Na.

To hasten the macrobiotic cure, drink as little as possible so that if you are a woman you urinate only twice in 24 hours — three times in the same period for a man.

About Chewing

Mahatma Gandhi said: You should chew your drinks and drink your foods.

One should chew each teaspoonful of food at least 50 times. If you wish to absorb the macrobiotic philosophy faster and reach a higher standard of health as soon as possible, chew each mouthful even more. A hundred to 150 times. Some foods — grains in particular — become more tasteful if you chew them well.

On the other hand, the more you chew a beefsteak the more tasteless it becomes. The sensory pleasure is largely in the memory of the smell and the sizzle and the sauce.

Food that is really good and necessary for the body becomes more tasteful as one loses the habit of wolfing food in great gulps and as one acquires the natural habit of chewing well. You will find in the simple foods delights you will not give up to the end of your life.

Digestion of cereals and other starches begins in the mouth. Chewing well is excellent exercise and more important, it forces one to pay attention to and be aware of what one is doing — to remember that the taking of nourishment

175

is a vital and sacred act. The entire meal ought to be eaten with gratitude, joyful thankfulness and utmost calm.

In the Orient for thousands of years, the taking of nourishment was a sacred act. In other times and in other places even today, men still have this attitude of great respect for their food. Some farmers, who are close to the elements and the vegetable realm, instinctively sense the importance of the daily repast and give to the act of eating the attention and respect it merits.

About Principal Foods

One of the most important discoveries in the history of man — ranking with the use of fire and salt — was the discovery of a basic food, the backbone of the daily diet, the staff of life. It had ramifications through the whole range of human activity: biological, physiological, geographical, political and economic.

In the Orient, especially the Far East, the concept of a basic food was considered the foundation of life. The basic food (grains) was deified in the beginning of history. Rice, wheat, barley, buckwheat, millet, oats, all these grains were cultivated in the Orient from prehistoric times, when they were considered sacred and holy plants.

One of the strangest things I find in Western nations is that this concept of grains as a basic food has virtually disappeared — except in the random package advertising of the breakfast-food companies who have created an industry out of the chemical treatment and Yin-izing of rice, wheat, oats and other grains.

Some special dishes — in many cases adapted by American macrobiotic cooks from original recipes devised by myself and my wife — will be given below. They have been culled from the cookbook which is described at the end of this book. They are designed to establish a healthy equilibrium in your physical constitution, neutralizing too much Yang and too much Yin — the latter being the greatest danger. They are also adapted to the experience of American friends who have learned how to avoid the entire range of foods on the American market which have been subjected to organized contamination through the use of insecticides, chemical fertilizers and chemical processing.

Macrobiotics is not the kind of vegetarianism which is merely sentimental. If animal foods are to be avoided, it is for the purpose of preserving and improving man's ability *to think*. Animal flesh is ideal for animals. Animal glands produce hormones which are good for animals, unaccustomed to thinking. Their center of sensitivity, however, is not at all developed like ours.

With the concept of a basic food and that of subsidiary foods clearly understood, the crucial five-to-one balance between Yin and Yang in the daily diet becomes manageable and possible. Without this concept, one ends up with his daily nourishment guided only by intermittent whims, fads and fancies — eating anything which happens to appeal to his senses at the moment, or indulges his feeling for affluence or fashion.

Soulfood

RICE   ORYZA SATIVA

Natural, whole, unpolished brown rice is the perfect food. For thousands of years, it has been the principal food of the most ancient civilizations of the Orient. It can be stored indefinitely without any chemical preservatives or refrigeration. The natural protective coating on each grain of rice is extraordinarily resistant to all chemicals, even sulfuric acid and acids in general. Each whole grain contains all the natural minerals, vitamins, proteins and lipides (organic compounds that make up the fats) necessary to the nutrition of man.

If you give an uneducated rat his choice between natural brown rice and the husked, polished, treated white rice, he will instinctively choose the former — never white rice. This basic instinct for survival, for saying "yes" to life, governs an animal's most crucial decision — what to eat. In Western man, this basic instinct has been dulled, if not lost, by years of flouting the basic laws of nature.

179

Some sixty years ago, after the invention of the German ("Engelberg") polishing machines which strip each grain of rice of its protective, transparent outer coating, so-called refined, polished, white rice came into fashion. These machines not only did what some people had previously done in threshing by hand; they did something worse — they stripped each grain of rice of its intermediate and inner shells as well, all of which contain precious minerals and nutrients. This "processing" of our perfect natural food has been extended further through pre-cooking and packaging, until little is left but the perishable hydrate of carbon core — stripped of its preservative hulls — which cannot be stored without the use of chemical additives.

Cooking your basic food, unpolished brown rice, will be one of the most challenging and rewarding experiences of your new regime. A heavy, modern pressure cooker — pressure being Yang — is a valuable and time-saving tool.

First, wash the brown rice thoroughly in cold water. To each cup of rice, add one to one-and-a-half cups of water in the pressure cooker — and a dash of sea-salt. You will discover the exact amount through trial and error. After the pressure cooker has come to a boil, turn it down on very low heat for 20 to 25 minutes and let it simmer. Then turn off the heat and let it stand for two to twenty minutes. Then remove the cover.

Next to a pressure cooker, the best utensil for cooking

rice is a heavy earthenware pot with a tight lid. This requires more time and, initially, more water: from two to three cups of water for each cup of rice. After the boiling point is reached, let the rice boil turbulently for five minutes, then turn down the heat so the water merely simmers for an hour or more.

Ideally, the rice is ready to serve when the grains at the bottom of the pot are slightly scorched. Scorched yellow or brown grains are the most Yang, the heaviest, richest in minerals and most nutritious. For this reason, sick people and Yin characters should have priority in eating from the bottom of the pot.

The amount of water, the amount of cooking time and the proper amount of salt — here is where trial and error can lead to art. It is always helpful to cook enough rice to last you and your family for one entire day or more. It will keep naturally without refrigeration and can easily be reheated. It is handy to have a pot of rice ready cooked always on the back of the stove. Even cold rice — dusted with sesame salt — or gomasio — can be very appetizing. Like most macrobiotic foods, plain brown rice may seem unappetizing the first time you taste it — especially if you have grown accustomed to heavily seasoned or elaborately sauced dishes. But, like all good things, it comes to taste more delicious the more it is chewed, and the more you eat of it. After a few days or weeks, you will wonder how you ever managed to live without it.

Cooking brown rice is merely the first challenge, then ingenuity can really be used. There are hundreds of ways of using cooked rice, in combination with other cereals, vegetables and sea food. After you have graduated from Regimen Number 7 and wish to experiment, there is a whole range of suggestions to inspire you to really creative cookery.

RICE CREAM   CRÈME DU RIZ GRILLE

For those who are especially ill, for those whose teeth are in no shape to give whole brown rice the proper mastication, as well as for those who live alone with limited cooking privileges, rice cream often makes the first ten days of an all-cereal regimen possible. It is obtainable in packages through macrobiotic channels. It takes less time to cook than whole rice and requires no more skill than heating a can of soup or a dish of commercial cereal. Rice cream can, however, be made at home merely by roasting rice in a pan or oven until it is golden brown. During the toasting the grains will pop like popcorn. Then the roasted rice can be ground to a meal or flour, either in a coffee grinder, with mortar and pestle or, if all else fails, in an electric blender. In either case, add four tablespoons of rice cream, to three cups of cold water, stir vigorously, add a dash of

seasalt, bring to a boil and let boil for about 20 minutes
— stirring it from time to time and adding water if necessary.
Rice cream prepared this way results in a thick soup or
porridge which may be served with toasted bread croutons
and dusted with gomasio.

To make a thick rice cream, with the consistency of
a pudding, add a tablespoonful of vegetable oil to an earthenware pot — the less oil the better. Heat the oil over a low
flame, then add a cup of rice cream. Roast the rice cream
for several minutes, stirring from time to time, until it
darkens and exudes a nut-like fragrance. Meanwhile prepare
two cups of boiling water. When the rice cream powder is
well roasted, add the first cup of boiling water. The mixture
will sputter and steam. By stirring it vigorously, you will end
up with a dough-like mixture in the center of the pot. Then
add the second cup of boiling water and a dash of seasalt.
Cover and continue cooking for another ten minutes. Stir
well to smoothen the mixture. Let it steam for another few
minutes, then serve. This rice cream pudding, dusted with
gomasio or chopped parsley, is delicious hot or cold. One
cup cooked this way amounts to three servings — enough
for an entire day for one person.

BUCKWHEAT   KASHA   BLE NOIR

This domesticated grass bearing a three-cornered fruit
is a native plant of Asia which has been grown in Europe

since the Middle Ages. In some sectors of Europe, Russia and Brittany for instance, buckwheat is a principal food, equivalent to rice in the Orient. Buckwheat is the most Yang of all cereals. Also it is the most readily available through ordinary commercial sources in unadulterated form — as kasha or as buckwheat flour. To cook kasha, saute a cup of the three-cornered grains in a tablespoonful of vegetable oil — safflower, olive or corn oil. Add two cups of water and one level teaspoon of seasalt. Let it boil slowly over a low flame until all the water has been absorbed and the grain is fluffy and dry. Some people like to mix kasha and rice; others take it straight. In any case kasha lends itself to almost as many creative urges as rice.

BUCKWHEAT CREAM   CRÈME DE SARRASIN

This is the equivalent of rice cream, only it is more Yang and has the advantage of being made out of pure buckwheat flour, more easily obtainable in its pristine state in the Western hemisphere than is brown rice. Cover the bottom of a pan with a tablespoon of oil — just enough to make a thin coating. Turn the heat on low and add two heaping tablespoons of buckwheat flour. Stir the flour steadily until it turns from beige to dark brown. Let it cool, then add from one to two cups of water and a dash of seasalt. Let it boil until it is thick. Once again the amount of water can be varied to suit your taste. It may be served in a soup bowl with croutons. It has the consistency, the appearance and something of the texture of black bean soup. After you have reestablished your health on the all-cereal regimen, you can experiment with buckwheat cream, using an onion soup stock — sautéed onions, water and soya sauce — instead of water. This gives it a much different taste. Through macrobiotic channels — and some Japanese shops in larger cities — you will also want to try later the delicious Japanese pasta or noodles made of buckwheat.

WHEAT   COUS COUS   CHAPATI

Wheat is one of the first cereals domesticated by man. It has been the white man's chief source of bread in Europe and America since the seventeenth century. But like rice, it has been the victim of industrial refining processes which reject the nutritious whole grain and use only the white hydrocarbon core. There is really only one commercial cereal on the U. S. market — WHEATENA — which preserves the natural food value of wheat.

In other areas of the world, like North Africa and India, whole wheat flour in its coarsest unrefined state is a principal food. CousCous is a staple of North African and Middle Eastern cooking, obtainable in the Arab quarter of most larger cities and sometimes in fancy gourmet shops or supermarkets where it is considered an exotic delicacy.

It is a coarse-grained wheat flour — Armenians call it boul-gour — which Arabs use as a base for a sauce of vegetables and meat. But it is delicious on its own. It may be steamed in a special utensil which the French call a *CousCouserie* or it may be boiled like kasha.

In India, chapati is a principal food, eaten every day. It is made with rough whole-wheat flour and is very good as a staple food for sick people and those who are very Yin. Add a small amount of salt to whole-wheat flour, knead it with water to form a soft dough. Take a tablespoonful of dough and make round balls, one at a time.

Roll them into thin round pieces and bake them in the oven. They may also be grilled on an open flame or heat and they will puff up as they bake. Chapati may also be rolled into small round pieces and fried in deep oil. They will puff up like ballons and are called Puri.

MILLET

Millet is among the most ancient of grains, grown since prehistoric times and used as a staple food in some parts of the world since biblical times and before. It is prepared much the same way as kasha. Sauté one cup of millet in two tablespoons of oil, add a little seasalt and two cups of water. Place over medium heat until it boils, then lower the heat and let it simmer until the grains thoroughly absorb the water, ending up fluffy and dry. Later, millet may be used in the same variety of ways as kasha.

Any of the American frontier breakfast dishes, oatmeal, cornmeal-mush, etc., may be used to vary the rice regimen in the first ten days. The only precaution is to make sure each cereal is in its pristine state and not processed with chemicals or additives of any kind. Buckwheat pancakes, another U. S. frontier breakfast, like the Brittany *crepes de sarrasin,* may be made by mixing buckwheat flour with whole-wheat flour; add a little salt, use water or tea instead of milk, and fry them on a griddle brushed with a small amount of vegetable oil.

RAW RICE

The most effective and speedy way of ridding the intestines, especially the duodenum, of all parasites is a simple and ancient Oriental prescription. Take a handful of raw rice in the morning instead of breakfast. Chew each mouthful at least a hundred times. If you do this for a few days you will be astonished at the results.

BREAD

Through macrobiotic channels in larger cities, and through some health-food shops, it is possible to obtain whole-wheat bread, guaranteed free of chemical additives, and in some cases made without yeast or other leavening. But in any case, you should know how to make your own bread. Mix four portions of whole-wheat flour with two portions of buckwheat flour, millet flour and corn meal (polenta): Add salt and a little oil and knead gently with water. Sometimes you may experiment by adding a little cooked rice. Oil small tart pans or a large bread pan and bake in the oven. Because no yeast or baking powder is used, do not expect the bread to be soft and light. Because no chemical preservatives are added, the bread will have to be kept in a cool place. But it is tasty when chewed well. By increasing the quantity of corn meal, you will have corn bread. Cold bread may taste better toasted or it may be sliced and fried in a tiny bit of oil.

GOMASIO   SESAME SALT

This is the indispensable condiment of the macrobiotic regimen. It makes possible a proper intake of salt without provoking thirst. Gomasio is obtainable through macrobiotic channels, but it is well to know how to make it yourself in any case. Because they are now in vogue as trimmings for bread and rolls in the U. S., sesame seeds are often obtainable in health-food shops and specialty shops. The proportion of seasalt to sesame seeds varies from one to four for adults and Yin people to one to five for children. Take one portion of seasalt, grind it in a *suribachi* (a ridged ceramic bowl with a wooden pestle) very quickly until it is powdered. Then toast it in a pan until it is sparkling.

Take four or five portions of sesame seeds, wash them and drain them. Then toast them quickly. A deep lightweight saucepan is best for quick shaking and to prevent the hot seeds from leaping out of the pan. As soon as they are toasted, grind them in the suribachi. They should crumble when crushed gently. If they taste raw, toast them a little more. Grind them gently the first time to make a coarse texture. Then add the salt and grind more finely. Grinding salt and sesame together covers each grain of salt with the natural oil of the seeds, to prevent provocation of thirst. When the mixture is ground in an electric blender, this protection is missing. Natural hand preparation is always superior to mechanical time-saving methods. Gomasio should be kept in a small bottle, hermetically sealed. It may be used as seasoning with every meal, over rice, buckwheat, any cereal. As you will discover later in this book, it may be taken by itself as a medicament — the dose is a spoonful.

UMEBOSHI PLUMS

In Japan, all traditional families make an annual ritual out of salting and conserving this Japanese plum which is never touched until at least three years after it is originally conserved. It is obtainable in macrobiotic centers and has a multitude of uses as food and as a medicament.

MISO AND SHOYU

Shoyu is the traditional Oriental sauce made by soya beans, wheat and salt, and fermented for at least three years. It is obtainable through macrobiotic channels. The commercial version of the traditional product is made with chemical short cuts and is to be avoided.

Miso is a paste made much the same way, of soya beans, wheat and salt. Both have a multitude of uses in the macrobiotic cuisine.

TAHINI

This delicacy is a paste or butter made out of crushed whole sesame seeds. It is a staple of Middle Eastern cuisine and may now be purchased at many specialty shops in the U. S., where it has become fashionable as a delicacy. It has many uses in the macrobiotic cuisine. But for someone beginning with Regimen Number 7, its principal use will be as an ingredient in Miso cream, a substitute spread for butter or cheese.

MISO CREAM

Take one big tablespoonful of miso and three tablespoonsful of Tahini — sesame butter. Add a tiny bit of water and mix thoroughly. The spread will turn out to have the consistency and something of the texture of peanut butter; but its exotic flavor is entirely original and will grow on you with each batch you mix. Spread on bread or rice crackers — obtainable through macrobiotic channels — it makes a hearty and portable picnic lunch for traveling or for eating on the job, with a tiny pocket-flask of hot tea for a chaser.

ABOUT TEA

In the Orient, tea is not just a beverage to be gulped down with ice cubes, laced with sugar or milk, squirted with lemon. It is, and has been for thousands of years, far more than a source of simple sensory pleasure, or for the slaking of thirst.

It is a very precious medicament, with its valued place in Oriental medicine — not one place, but a hundred places, as many as there are varieties of tea; Yin tea and Yang tea; simple green tea made of the roasted leaves and twigs no less than three years of age; immensely complicated blends composed of ginseng and as many as fifteen other medicinal plants combined.

The cultivation and blending of tea, its preparation, the amount served, the manner in which it is brewed and offered, all this is controlled by the most ancient ceremonies and traditions. Tea is, at its root, a religion unto itself — as so beautifully explained in *The Book of Tea,* by the Japanese author, Okakura.

Tea properly cultivated, properly selected, appropriately brewed and served, and drunk under propitious circumstances in small amounts, can be a revelation. It can be something quite beyond the chemical tranquilizers now in vogue. It can be something to sharpen our senses, intensify our awareness, uplift our judgment and deepen our planes of meditation — not just another mélange of tastes to provide fleeting sensory pleasure.

The less liquid one drinks, the more important it then becomes that it be perfectly prepared and served in a way which helps us to break compulsive old habits of drinking just for the sake of drinking. Tea should be served in the tiniest cups that can be found. And it should be served as hot as possible. A tiny Japanese saki cup full of boiling hot tea properly prepared can be more satisfying than a huge cup full of the "instant" variety laced with sugar and cream, or a tea bag laced with carcinogenic dye to give each brew the uniform color.

And remember: Tea is never served or meant to be drunk during a meal. It is the final course of each meal — to be enjoyed by and for itself.

There are no instant ways of making tea properly. It will take ten to twenty minutes to prepare tea properly, although all teas mentioned here can be kept indefinitely and reheated.

Forget about your fancy China teapots. What you will need is a small metal Japanese teapot in which tea can be boiled and served. Failing that, an enamel teakettle big enough to hold 32 ounces of water is the next best bet. As an interim measure, tea can be brewed in an enamel sauce-pan. Aluminum and iron are to be avoided if possible.

COARSE GREEN TEA   BANCHA
THE DE TROIS ANS

The texture and appearance of this tea will seem strange at the beginning. It looks like dried leaves and twigs, mostly wood, because all the leaves are at least three years old. Put a small amount in a pan and roast it over a medium flame for a few minutes until it smokes or turns dark brown. It may be roasted slowly and sometimes more effectively in an open pan in the oven with a low heat. Immerse the smoking charred remains in 24 ounces of cold water. Bring it to a boil and let it boil for ten minutes. You will discover in time the proper amount of tea to use to suit your taste. If it seems to have little color at first, it may mean it has not been sufficiently roasted, or you have not used enough tea. Try again. A batch of tea, sufficient for several pots, may be roasted and kept in a sealed jar.

SOYA BAN   COARSE GREEN BANCHA TEA WITH SOY SAUCE

Take a small teacup and pour enough soya sauce to amount to one-tenth of its capacity. Add boiling-hot coarse green bancha tea and serve. Strange as the mixture sounds, it will taste like the most hearty and delicious bouillon. It is marvelous as a pick-up when you are tired at the end of the day. It works wonders on skeptical friends who have done too much drinking (of alcohol) and are willing to try anything as an antidote to a hangover. A cup of soya ban the night before will head off any hangover and any skeptic may be more amenable the morning after to other "miraculous" aspects of the macrobiotic regimen.

MU TEA   THE MU

This is the most Yang of beverages. It contains the legendary herb ginseng — the most Yang of all herbs used to make tea and fifteen other medicinal plants: peony; root of Angelica; sea thistle; carthanne; rush; ginger; hoelen; japonica; licorice; cinnamon; bitter orange rind; rehmanial radix; moutan cortex; carophyll flos and persical semen. The word *mu* means space or infinity in Japanese, and Mu tea is so named because it is the beverage for development of superior judgment. It is usually obtainable only through macrobiotic channels and comes in small packages.

Open a package and pour the Mu tea into 32 ounces of cold water. Bring it to a boil and let it boil from five to ten minutes. Here again you will discover for yourself what amount of boiling best suits your taste. If the Mu tea is being prepared for someone who is very Yin, the water should be boiled away to make the tea stronger — until there remains merely 16 to 20 ounces of the original 32. This will be enough for two days. It can, of course, be reheated each time it is served. Mu tea is another delicious and exotic introduction to macrobiotic foods for friends and skeptics who have tried everything — from *cannabis sativa* to *d-lysergic acid diethylamide*. For children who need to be withdrawn gradually from orange juice and other sugared drinks, Mu tea can be spiked with a few drops of natural unsugared apple juice. Give them less and less apple juice in their tea until they come to appreciate the delicious Mu flavor completely on its own.

LOTUS TEA   KOHREN TEA

This tea is made of dried shaved lotus root, usually obtainable in bulk through macrobiotic channels. Take one teaspoonful, add a small cup of hot water, stir vigorously while drinking. It is a marvelous remedy for coughs — including whooping cough and asthmatic coughs — and in that case should be taken three times each day to the exclusion of all other liquids.

LOTUS TEA

Take two inches of raw lotus root — usually obtainable in Oriental districts or markets — squeeze out the juice; add ten per cent of crushed raw ginger and a little salt. Add a cup of boiling water. It is also very effective against coughs and as a medicament for people who are too Yin.

MINT TEA

Pick fresh mint leaves in season and let them dry. The dried leaves may be kept for years. Many health-food shops also stock dried mint leaves. Take a few dried mint leaves and add them to a few ounces of boiling water. Let them steep for at least five minutes. You will learn to adjust the strength to suit individual tastes. Mint tea may be weak and delicate or — as it is reheated or boiled again — dark and strong. With the addition of a tiny amount of seasalt, it makes a good breakfast drink.

THYME TEA

Fresh or dried thyme can be used to give delicious flavor to tea in the same manner as mint.

OTHER BEVERAGES

OHSAWA COFFEE

This is a blend of various cereals — available through macrobiotic channels — developed as a coffee substitute. Add one teaspoonful of Yannoh to 15 ounces of cold water and let it boil for ten minutes. Adventurous souls may try to make the coffee-blend themselves. Here is the formula: take three tablespoons of rice, two of wheat and one each of aduki beans, chick peas and chicory. Roast each of them separately until they are well browned. Then mix them together and brown in a pan with one tablespoon of oil. Let cool and grind into a powder. *Voila.*

DANDELIO

This is another coffee substitute — available through macrobiotic channels — whose principal ingredient is dandelion roots — the same dandelion whose flowers were used to make wine in the U. S. during Prohibition. Add one teaspoon of dandelio for each cup of water and boil for ten minutes, strain and serve. To make the blend yourself, pick dandelions, using only the root. Wash them and let them dry. Cut them into small pieces, brown in a pan with a little oil, then grind in a coffee grinder. Chicory may be added for those who prefer a more bitter taste.

KOKOH

This is a blend of various cereals into a cereal milk product. It is available through macrobiotic channels, fortunately, for to make it oneself could be quite a chore. Its ingredients are roasted rice, glutinous rice, oatmeal, soya beans and sesame seeds. Add one heaping tablespoon of kokoh to 11 ounces of water, stir well and boil for ten minutes. It is a tasty and easily prepared substitute for breakfast. Also, as you will discover when you reach the stage of creative experimentation in your kitchen, it can be used in desserts, puddings, and is superb for coating deep-fried foods. A coating of rice cream or Kokoh gives deep-fried foods a mysterious, exotic, sealing texture that will baffle any gourmet.

KUZU

Some people favor this as a pickup, swearing it beats any alcoholic cocktail. Others find the texture too strange for their taste and consider it a medicine. In either case, it has myriad uses. It is a white powder made of arrowroot, nature's own vegetal gelatin, which can be used to create an instant clear sauce or gravy for many dishes, varying only the flavoring. Take one heaping teaspoon of kuzu powder and let it dissolve in two or three teaspoons of cold water. Add ten ounces of water and boil the mixture until it becomes clear, transparent and it thickens. Add a little shoyu sauce and it will have the taste and texture of a clear cream soup, with the flavor of a hearty bouillon.

UMEBOSHI JUICE

This is one of the rare macrobiotic beverages that one can drink cold. Umeboshi plums are available through macrobiotic channels. In some cities with Oriental populations they are available elsewhere and are known as Chinese salt plums. Take one plum and boil it in two pints of water for several minutes until the plum disintegrates. Strain it or leave it as it is, according to your taste. Add two more pints of water and let it cool. It is ideal as a summer drink, with a flavor all its own.

UME SYO KUZU

This is the *piece de resistance* among macrobiotic medicinal beverages — combining three valuable ingredients. Take one umeboshi plum, crush it in a half pint of cold water. Add one heaping teaspoon of kuzu powder. Then add one teaspoon of grated ginger and another pint of water. Boil the mixture until it becomes clear and thickens, then add a small dash of shoyu sauce to each portion as you drink it. It does wonders in knocking out a cold.

ADUKI JUICE

Aduki beans are small red beans available through macrobiotic channels. Boil one tablespoon of aduki beans in two quarts of water until half the liquid has boiled away. Add a pinch of salt. This brew is very good for those with kidney troubles.

RADISH DRINK I

Take a white radish — *daikon* — and grate it fine. Add two tablespoons of grated radish to one and a half pints of hot water. Mix in two tablespoons of shoyu sauce and one teaspoon of grated ginger root. This is very good for colds. Drink it in bed and it will help you to perspire or urinate and bring down any fever.

RADISH DRINK II

Grate a white radish — *daikon* — and squeeze out the juice. Take one fourth of a pint of radish juice, add a half pint of water and a little seasalt and boil for a few minutes. This is good for swelling in the legs but should never be taken more than once a day and never for more than three days in succession.

SPECIAL RICE CREAM

Roast half a pint of raw, brown, unpolished rice in a pan until it is golden brown. Boil it in two quarts of water for an hour or two. Strain through a cotton cloth. This is a good tonic or late afternoon pickup and a fine breakfast for sick people.

RICE TEA

Whole, brown, unpolished rice may also be used to make tea. Roast the rice until golden brown. For each tablespoon of rice add ten times the amount of water and bring it to a boil. Add a little salt and serve. Roasted rice and roasted bancha tea may be mixed together and used to make a beverage. The roasted rice may be strained out and eaten by itself as a staple food.

WHEAT TEA

Grains of wheat may also be used to make a beverage — another one of those rare macrobiotic drinks which can be served cold. Roast grains in a pan or in the oven until they are brown. Boil one heaping teaspoonful in five ounces of water to make the tea.

The Oneness of the Universe

The sky seems starless in the blaze of noon. The brilliance of millions of suns and numberless stars can only be seen through the dark of night. Light can only be seen through the darkness. Beauty stands out amid ugliness. There are no wise men in a wise nation. An honest man is blissfully unaware of his virtue. A man who is healthy does not know what health is.

If you think you possess courage, honesty, justice, patience, health, you are apt to be a stranger to these qualities.

Freedom can be found in slavery. Happiness can be found in the depths of misfortune. Health can be attained through the most agonizing illness. Health established with the aid of medicines is transitory, dependent and uncertain, compared to the natural well-being of even the tiniest animal.

True health can be maintained even under the most miserable of circumstances, as soldiers at the front have shown us. And disease can flourish in the most affluent, protected, pampered and over-sanitized way of life.

True health can only be established by individual triumph over the constant temptations and dangers of daily life. It cannot be established through a proxy war on cancer, war on poverty, war on tuberculosis or war on heart disease. True health can be won by recognition of the principle of the Oneness of the universe, and man's relation to it. Total destruction of the forces that create disease would be suicidal — as for example in the uses of insecticides, poisoning foods as well as so-called destructive insects; upsetting the balance of nature.

There can be no good without evil; no beauty without ugliness. There can be no front without a back. Freedom can be found only through discipline. The loveliest lotus flower grows in the dirtiest mud. Liberty only has significance in the midst of oppression and travail.

Liberty which is planned, legislated, bestowed on others, is no liberty at all. Peace maintained by law is not peace at all. Fighting for the freedom of others sometimes appears to be noble and alluring; but true freedom cannot be bestowed on others. Trying to do so merely obstructs the flowering of man's innate faculty, his own desire and will for freedom. Freedom can only be established by oneself for oneself. A strong, free, faithful and admirable man can live happily even in the midst of violence and vicissitudes. Only in the deepest morass of troubles is he able to display the whole of his unlimited range of fortitude: outwardly very Yin, calm, silent, open, profound, receptive, but inwardly very Yang, strong and absolutely independent. That is the true man.

Let us, then accept the universe; say "yes" to life, accept misfortune as well as welcome happiness. Disease and health, war and peace, foe and friend, death and life, poverty and riches, are all part of a grand design.

Everything that happens to us provides some experience or develops some quality in our character that has been hidden or missing. Everything that appears as an unbearable adversity can be converted into an ally. He who can embrace his antagonists is the happiest among men.

Accept everything with the greatest pleasure and thanks and give everything with the greatest pleasure and gratitude. Give and give without mental reservation. If you give something that can be replaced, that is no gift at all. Real giving means depriving oneself of something that is most precious, most necessary and most important: life itself — part of it or all.

The English word "sacrifice" is a conception generally admired, seldom practiced, and very deceiving. I do not recommend it to you. But the gift of life can be shared with others by teaching the Unique Principle of Yin/Yang. Never with words, but with deeds.

Your ability to accept everything and to give everything will be your yardstick, your private thermometer that will always reveal to you — and you alone — the true state of your health.

Let macrobiotics become your way of life. Give food and drink their proper place, no more. Do not shed one set of chains and take on another. Work hard, tire yourself physically. Don't allow yourself to become pampered or spoiled, or it will work adversely on the energy produced by your healthy diet.

If you have been able to re-establish your health by being your own doctor, if you have begun to contemplate, no matter how shakily, new horizons of life, I would be grateful if you would send me a short history of your experience with macrobiotics. One never knows how or when his experience in healing himself may encourage other people. This is the first step in a new life. Try to share your experience with your friends and neighbors — your former enemies, especially if they are suffering as you suffered. Try to show them, through your example, the simplicity and the superiority of the macrobiotic way to health and happiness.

If you fail to do this, it means you are not completely healthy yet. You are still exclusive, antagonistic, antisocial, arrogant. You are still *sanpaku* and you will fall again.

Exclusiveness is the most difficult of all diseases and the source of untold unhappiness. You must really become the kind of man or woman who cannot really dislike another human being.

You must learn to love again and to love means to give and give and never take in return. The give-and-take system is merely well-organized egotism. To give is to become a creator.

Everything you think you own will be lost to you sooner or later anyway. What begins, ends. To give and to give, without limit, means you have opened an account in the unlimited bank, the bank of Infinity, an insurance company, unlike ordinary insurance companies, which can guarantee infinite life to you. The only premium you pay is to continue giving. Giving what? That which is most precious to you: health and happiness; the keys to the kingdom. These keys are merely the simple act of communicating — through deeds and not words — comprehension of the Unique Principle of Yin/Yang and the macrobiotic art of longevity and rejuvenation.

Health and happiness can become as contagious as disease. And those who help spread this contagion will find joy unto the end of their days.

One cannot expect to attain supreme judgment in an instant of insight. One must increasingly suffer heat, cold, hunger and the greatest of difficulties as he grows older. *Vivere Parvo* — live a poor, humble and struggling life and you will find untold richness.

Man can be inferior to the animals, but he has within him the possibility to become profoundly human and even divine.

MACROBIOTIC TABLE OF DAILY FOOD
IN ORDER OF YIN ▽ TO YANG △

▽ SUGAR   CEREALS

FRUITS   FISH

DAIRY   EGGS

NUTS   △ ANIMAL MEAT

VEGETABLES

FRUITS

▽ ▽ ▽ PINEAPPLE   LIME

PAPAYA   MELON

MANGO   WALNUT

GRAPEFRUIT   ALMOND

ORANGE   ▽ OLIVE

BANANA   HAZEL NUT

LEMON   WATERMELON

FIG   △ STRAWBERRY

PEAR   CHERRY

PEANUT   APPLE

CASHEW   △ △ CHESTNUT

PEACH

DAIRY PRODUCTS

▽ ▽ ▽ YOGURT   ▽ CAMEMBERT

    SWEET SOUR CREAM   DUTCH CHEESE (EDAM)

    CREAM   GRUYERE

    BUTTER   ROCQUEFORT

    CREAM CHEESE   △ △ GOAT'S MILK

  ▽ ▽ MILK   GOAT CHEESE

VEGETABLES

▽ ▽ ▽ EGGPLANT   CAULIFLOWER

    TOMATO   KALE

    POTATO   ENDIVE

    MUSHROOM   CHICK PEAS

    SWEET POTATO   CHICORY

    YAM   ESCAROLE

    PEPPERS   PARSLEY

    ASPARAGUS   △ DANDELION

    BEAN SPROUTS   BEETS

    ARTICHOKE   PARSNIPS

    CUCUMBER   ONION

    STRING BEANS   RADISH

  ▽ ▽ GREEN PEAS   GARLIC

    BEANS (EXCEPT ADUKI) △ △ PUMPKIN

    CHINESE CABBAGE   CARROT

    SOUR GRASS (SHAV)   LEEK

    RHUBARB   TURNIP (LONG)

    ZUCCHINI   COLTSFOOT

    CELERY   WATERCRESS

    LENTIL   SALSIFIE

  ▽ CABBAGE   DANDELION ROOT

                       △ △ △ BURDOCK ROOT

CEREALS

▽ CORN	MILLET
RYE	WHEAT
BARLEY	△ RICE
OATS	△ △ BUCKWHEAT

FISH

▽ OYSTER	TROUT
CLAM	SOLE
OCTOPUS	△ SALMON
EEL	SHRIMP
CARP	HERRING
MUSSEL	SARDINE
HALIBUT	RED SNAPPER (TAI)
LOBSTER	△ △ CAVIAR

ANIMALS

▽ ▽ SNAIL	△ PIGEON
FROG	PARTRIDGE**
PORK	DUCK
BEEF	TURKEY**
HORSE	△ △ EGG*
HARE	△ △ △ PHEASANT**
▽ CHICKEN**	

*The egg must be a fertilized one.
**The chickens, turkeys and other fowl must be fed organic whole grain.

MISCELLANEOUS

▽ ▽ ▽ HONEY   OLIVE OIL

       MOLASSES   ▽ SUNFLOWER OIL

       GREASE   SAFFLOWER OIL

    ▽ ▽ COCOANUT OIL   △ SESAME OIL

       PEANUT OIL

DRINKS

▽ ▽ ▽ SOFT DRINKS   THYME TEA

       TEA (WITH DYESTUFF)   HERB TEAS

       COFFEE   MUGWORT TEA

       CHOCOLATE   △ BANCHA TEA

       CHAMPAGNE   KOKOH

       WINE   CHICORY

       FRUIT JUICE   DANDELIQ

    ▽ ▽ BEER   YANNOH

       SODA   △ △ MU TEA

     ▽ MINERAL WATER   KUZU

       DEEP WELL WATER   UMEBOSHI JUICE

       MINT TEA   △ △ △ GINSENG

All food and drinks in these tables must be naturally grown, never artificially or industrially prepared. One must be careful, for so many products such as chickens, eggs, turkeys are chemically fed. Yin/Yang also varies according to the season and climate of origin and, of course, can be changed in the process of cooking and preparation.

PHYSICAL PHENOMENA   YIN/YANG TABLE

	YIN	**YANG**
TENDENCY	EXPANSION	CONSTRICTION
POSITION	OUTWARD	INWARD
STRUCTURE	SPACE	TIME
DIRECTION	ASCENT	DESCENT
COLOR	PURPLE	RED
TEMPERATURE	COLD	HOT
WEIGHT	LIGHT	HEAVY
FACTOR	WATER	FIRE
ATOMIC	ELECTRON	PROTON
ELEMENT	POTASSIUM	SODIUM
	O, P, CA, O, etc.	H, As, Cl, Na, Mg only

BIOLOGICAL AND PHYSIOLOGICAL

BIOLOGICAL	VEGETABLE	ANIMAL
AGRICULTURAL	SALAD	CEREAL
SEX	FEMALE	MALE
NERVES	SYMPATHETIC	PARA-SYMPATHETIC
BIRTH	COLD SEASON	HOT SEASON
MOVEMENT	FEMININE	MASCULINE
TASTE	HOT (CURRY)-SOUR-SWEET	SALTY BITTER
VITAMINS	C	D K

BIO-ECOLOGICAL

COUNTRY OF ORIGIN	TROPICAL	FRIGID
SEASON	SUMMER	WINTER

Biographical Note

Sakurazawa-Ohsawa

SAKURAZAWA NYOITI was born October 18, 1893 in Kyoto, Japan. He is better known in Europe and America by his Westernized name George Ohsawa. In Japanese Ohsawa has the same meaning as Sakurazawa: a pool surrounded by flowering cherry trees.

Family tragedy and near-fatal illness came to him at an early age and began his compulsive search for the ancient secrets of Oriental medicine. His mother was a nurse and midwife trained in the techniques of Western medicine who, like so many families in Japan at the beginning of the 20th century, broke with ancient tradition and accepted Western ideas of medicine, nourishment, technology and even religion. When his mother died — abandoned as incurable by the Western medicine she had espoused — when two sisters and a brother died the same way, and when the ten-year old Sakurazawa was told he was incurably ill of tuberculosis and ulcers at the age of ten, he rebelled and began the study of ancient Oriental medicine which had been officially outlawed by the Japanese government under the impact of modernization.

After he had worked out his own salvation, he decided to dedicate the rest of his life to the study of the medicine which had saved him. He was attracted to the career of a famous Japanese practitioner, Sagan Isiduka, who had discovered the biochemical validity of the ancient Unique Principle of Yin/Yang when he uncovered the complementary antagonism between sodium (Na) and potassium (K). Isiduka was able to cure thousands of patients — many of them abandoned as incurable by the new medicine from the West. He was so well known in his time that any letter addressed to "Dr. Anti-Doctor, Tokyo" was automatically delivered to him. When he died his funeral escort was two miles long.

Sakurazawa undertook intensive study of the discoveries of Isiduka and, in time, went beyond them to become, in effect, his heir and successor. He submerged himself in years of research and study of ancient Indian medicine, ancient Chinese medicine as well as their philosophical underpinnings, going back to the sacred books of the most ancient of civilizations. After World War I he undertook the study of Western medicine and science at the Sorbonne and the Pasteur Institute in Paris. To support himself in France, he began the private practice of acupunture, then virtually unknown in Europe. Although acupuncture is, to him, like chemical medications a symptomatic treatment, completely inferior to other Oriental medicinal ideas, its "miraculous" results appealed to "simplistically inclined Europeans" and it enjoyed a great surge of popularity due to the collaboration of Soilie de Morant who tirelessly spread its techniques in France and Germany long after Sakurazawa had left Europe.

Sakurazawa-Ohsawa is also credited with introducing to France the philosophy of "Do" underlying both "Kado" — flower arrangement — and "Judo." To his increasing consternation, Europe has made a vogue of the superficial techniques of flower arrangement and jiujitsu, completely passing over the underlying philosophy of Do — the Unique Principle of Yin/Yang out of which they breathe and bloom.

It was in reading *The Primitive Mind* by the French sociologist and Member of the Academy of Science Levy-Bruhl, that young Sakurazawa finally realized the dimensions of the gulf separating Western thought from Eastern philosophy. He was astonished to discover that the eminent French scientist had, he felt, completely missed the point of the so-called primitive mentality.

"I should know," Sakarazawa-Ohsawa insists, "for if anyone had a primitive mentality, it was I." He went straight to the Sorbonne to confront Levy-Bruhl and explain to him where he had gone astray in his writings. Levy-Bruhl did not dispute the fact that a wall of incomprehension separated them and suggested that the young Japanese should try to bridge it from the other side by writing a book himself.

"If I had known then what I know now, I probably would never have gone near the Professor," Sakurazawa-Ohsawa admits today. "I understood the word *primitive* as something completely basic, laudatory, even honorable. I had no idea it was a term of opprobrium in the West."

At any rate this encounter resulted in publication of Sakurazawa's first book: *Principe Unique de la Philosophie et de la Science d'Extreme Orient* published in 1931 by the Librarie Philosophique J. Vrin, 6 Place de la Sorbonne, Paris.

In the next four decades Sakurazawa-Ohsawa published some 300 works in Japanese and more than 20 books in Western languages, principally French. In a preface to a recent work he confessed to being "very very ashamed. I have written too much, explained too much. What a waste of paper and ink. I must stop. Buddha never wrote a line. Lao-Tse limited himself to 83 phrases. The Maha Prajna Hridaya Paramita Sutra (the great sacred book of India) employs less than 300 words to unveil the entire secret of the universe."

Sakurazawa-Ohsawa confides to friends his belief that he will die at an early age — perhaps when he is 85 — for having wasted so many words. But trying to bridge the gap between West and East with words sometimes seems impossible. Words and concepts which exist in one language simply do not exist in another and "our conception of the world is completely different and diametrically opposed to that of the West."

Sakurazawa-Ohsawa has found that sometimes Western readers comprehend his simple ideas years — even decades — after they have first read them. Then they besiege him with letters testifying to their awesome sense of belated discovery.

In 1940 Sakurazawa-Ohsawa published three books in Japan in which he prophesied the death of Gandhi, the end of British rule in India, the complete defeat of Japan for the first time in 2600 years and, incidentally, the decline and fall of the American world empire. (After his first visits to the United States he concluded that the decline had already begun with the deterioration of the physical health of the American people.)

His prophecy of the defeat of Japan — made only a few months before Pearl Harbor — almost cost him his life after he was imprisoned in Japan.

After the war, when he was over fifty years old, he took leave of his home, his books, his typewriter. His wife Lima — a professor of traditional Japanese music — left behind her precious musical instruments and together they began an odyssey that took them to most countries of the Western world.

"I had heard the despairing cry of official Western medicine myself and I could not stay indifferent any more," he explains.

In India, the United States, South America, Africa and Europe he held small seminars designed to guide foreigners to an understanding of the Unique Principle, teaching the way to health and happiness through correct eating and drinking. In the wake of his travels, small groups of dedicated followers continued the study and application of his ideas.

Sakurazawa has always discouraged any formal organization of a world movement with himself as its leader. He abjured any title except the simple appellation *Sensei* or Guide. Centers of Information of his ideas and theories are called, at his insistence, Centres Ignoramus out of respect and admiration for the 19th century German psychologist Emile du Bois-Reykond, who declared at the end of his life: "Ignoramus, Ignoramibus," Latin for "We know nothing, we will never know anything."

In Europe friends of Sakurazawa-Ohsawa have established restaurants, summer camps and multiple outlets for his publications and for staple foods organically grown in accord with his philosophy. Farms and factories in Belgium, France (and now in Chico, California as well) produce macrobiotic foods and drinks. Hundreds of health food shops in Europe — and some in the United States — handle products first introduced by Sensei Sakurazawa-Ohsawa. When he first visited France after World War I, there was virtually no rice cultivation in Europe at all. Now unpolished brown rice is raised and marketed annually in increasing amounts each year.

In 1964 — as a result of the pioneer work of the French biochemist L. Kervran, author of the work *Biological Transmutation,* Sakurazawa-Ohsawa collaborated with Kervran and in subsequent experiments in Tokyo in January he accomplished the first transmutation of sodium (Na) into potassium (K) under low temperature without high pressure. He repeated the feat before a selected audience of the Japanese Diet in July, 1964. Sakurazawa-Ohsawa sees the ramifications of this breakthrough as occupying the remainder of his life.

SELECTED BIBLIOGRAPHY

SAKURAZAWA-OHSAWA

FRENCH

Le Principle Unique de la Philosophie et de la Science d'Extreme Orient
Vrin Paris   1931
Le Livre des Fleurs   Plon   Paris   1932
La Medecine Chinoise   Le Francois   Paris   1934
Le Livre du Judo   Sekai Seihu   Tokyo   1952
Jack et Madame Mitie (Deux Erewhoniens dans la Jungle dite "Civilization")
E D Paris   1956
La Philosophie de la Medecine d'Extreme Orient   Vrin   Paris   1956
Zen Macrobiotique   ID M   Bruxelles   1961
Acupuncutre Macrobiotique   Sesam   Paris   1961

ENGLISH

Two Great Indians in Japan   Centre Ignoramus Calcutta   India   1954

JAPANESE

Macrobiotics
History of China From 2000 B.C. Until Today
Franklin   A physiological and biological biography
Gandhi   A physiological and biological biography
Clara Schumann and Her Father   A physiological and biological Study
The Encounter Between East and West by F.S.C. Northrup
Translation and Critique

Man the Unknown   by Alexis Carrell   Translation and Critique
The Fatality of Science

Index